CREATED To WIN!

12 Keys To True Success

KEVIN BAERG

Created To Win!

12 Keys To True Success
Kevin Baerg

Most of this book was formerly published and copyrighted in 1996 under the title **"Created for Excellence."** (Complete with Scripture References).

Cover design by cm design works
Front cover photo © 1999 by PhotoDisc, Inc.
Portrait by Van Ostrom Photography
Printing by Data Reproductions Corporation
Printed in the United States of America

First printing: April, 1999

ISBN 00-9649090-2-2 (Hardcover)
ISBN 00-9649090-1-4 (Softcover)

Inspiration Press

P.O. Box 44604 ◆ Tacoma, WA 98444-0604 ◆ 1-800-539-2350
Amvox: 253-596-8077 ◆ www.inspiration4u.com

ACKNOWLEDGMENTS

As I reflect on the completion of this project, I wish to thank the many people who have helped make my vision a reality.

Thanks go first to my parents, grandparents, and all my relatives for encouraging me to have faith and be the best I could be.

To my wife, Patty, and our children, Sarah and Tim — your love means more than you know. Thank you for supporting me in so many ways during the long months this has taken.

To all our friends at church: Pastor Bill and Marj Wolfson, the Staff and Board, and so many others — your "How's the book coming" questions and encouragement have helped fuel my fire.

To Bob Moawad and our friends at Edge Learning Institute: I learned many of the concepts and principles in this book while working with you — thank you. Special thanks to Dick Anderson for being a mentor to me.

To the leadership of Youth With a Mission: Loren Cunningham, Floyd McClung and so many others — thanks for the incredible foundation for godliness and opportunities for service you gave a young man nearly 20 years ago. I worked with Peter Warren for almost seven years — you impacted my life bro! John Dawson — you've always been an inspiration to me — thanks for everything. If you ever need to be encouraged, call Andy Zimmermann, my closest friend — I love you like a brother!

To all the behind-the-scenes folk who helped me in various ways and answered my many questions — thanks! This includes: John White, Dick Payne, Rachael Costner, Mary Pugliese, Colin Magnuson, Jim Vitzthum, Bryan Lovely, Bret Van Ostrom, and Tim Wertheimer.

To all the great teachers and authors who have influenced my life, belief, strategy and skill — thank you for letting me stand on your shoulders.

To everyone else who has had an impact on my life — thank you. You've helped make me who I am. I couldn't have done this without you.

Last, but definitely not least, thank you to God for giving me life, a future and a hope. May he continue to mold me into the man he has planned for me to become.

*Dedicated to the excellence that lies dormant
within you. May God awaken it now!*

*Most of all to my precious wife, Patty, who is a living,
shining example of unconditional love,
forgiveness and support. I love you honey.*

*And to our wonderful children, Sarah and Tim.
May all our dreams as a family continue to come true!*

TABLE OF CONTENTS

Introduction 7

1. The Engine that Powers Your Dreams
   — *Defining Your Vision* 9

2. The Building Blocks of Character
   — *Clarifying & Aligning Your Values* 25

3. Breaking Glass Ceilings
   — *Identifying & Changing Your Limiting Beliefs* 39

4. You Are What You Think You Are
   — *Increasing Performance by Raising Expectations* 51

5. The Awesome Power of Your Tongue
   — *Speaking Words of Life* 63

6. Know Whose You Are
   — *Discovering the Image You Are Molded In* 77

7. The Wind Beneath Your Wings
   — *Gaining Altitude with a Rising Attitude* 91

8. Evidence of Things Unseen
   — *Using The Dynamic Duo of Faith & Imagination* 103

9. Create a Compelling Future
   — *Harnessing the Power of Goal-Setting* 119

10. Lights, Camera...Action!
    — *Developing & Implementing Your Action Plan* 139

11. Maximize Your Resources
    — *Taking Control of Your Time & Treasure* 155

12. The Key to Lasting Happiness
    — *Building Loving Relationships* 175

Appendix 187

To every person there comes that special moment when you are tapped on the shoulder to do a very special thing unique to you. What a tragedy if that moment finds you unprepared for the work that would be your finest hour.

— *Winston Churchill*

Introduction

"And now I will show you the most
excellent way."

Excellence...is that what you really
want? Take a moment to think about it.
Do you strongly desire to reach your
full potential? If in your heart there is a resound-
ing, "Yes!" — then I firmly believe this book will
help you in your quest.

Far too many people accept life the way it
comes to them and assume it is "their destiny"
instead of actively pursuing God and his
purposes for their life. 'Created To Win' is a
system of principles you can use everyday to
grow into the person God created you to be and
achieve *true success*.

*"Unhappiness is in
not knowing what
we want and killing
ourselves to get it."*
— Don Herold

My premise in writing this book is that first of
all, I truly believe that God has a plan and a
purpose for **everyone** on this planet — *and
they are good plans!* Secondly I am convinced
that *God really wants you to succeed!*

What is success? I believe the true definition
of success is simply fulfilling the purposes for
which God has created you. Of course, this
requires that you discover what this purpose is
and then begin to pursue it with "reckless
abandon!"

Perhaps you are reading this book to become
more motivated, or maybe someone else wants
you to turn it up a notch! I like to tell the
following story about motivation:

A man took a shortcut through a graveyard
one night and promptly fell in a freshly dug
grave. Try as he might, he couldn't find a way
out. He finally resigned himself to this fact and
waited for morning and the possibility of some

"No one keeps up his enthusiasm automatically. Enthusiasm must be nourished with new actions, new aspirations, new efforts, new vision. It is one's own fault if his enthusiasm is gone. He has failed to feed it."
— Anonymous

assistance. Wouldn't you know it, but another guy took the same shortcut and also fell in the hole. He too tried with no avail to climb out. Finally, just as the second man was getting ready to give up, a voice came from the corner behind him.

"It's no use, you can't get out!"

But at that moment he somehow *found a way out!* The second man had entered into a new level of motivation!

I believe you too can accomplish anything you set your mind to if you'll follow the unchanging principles in these pages.

I have attempted to make this book as practical and as 'hands on' in nature as my seminar. At the end of most chapters you will find a Personal Application section for you to complete. This will assist you in assimilating the concepts into your life and help increase your retention of the material.

Like anything in life, you get out only what you put in. In order to get the most out of this book, I urge you to invest the time necessary to complete the exercises. Some have chosen to read through the entire book first and then return to work on the personal application.

I have selected a layout that allowed me to liberally sprinkle pertinent quotes throughout each chapter. When no credit is given for a quote, it simply means I am not sure of its origin. I have collected these for years and unfortunately, not everyone is quoted or credited properly.

My hope and prayer is that you will take this information and use it to achieve the true success both you and God desire.

Have fun and enjoy the journey!

1 The Engine that Powers Your Dreams
— *Defining Your Vision*

"But the plans of the Lord stand firm
forever, the purposes of his heart
through all generations."

— Psalms

God has a vision for the entire
creation including a very special
plan just for you!

Your vision is the foundation for your life. I
challenge you to examine yourself — your
behavior today, tomorrow, next week, next
month and next year — in the context of what
truly matters most to you.

By keeping your vision in mind, you can
better ensure that whatever actions you take on
a specific day are in alignment with what you
have already decided is extremely important.
Each day can therefore contribute in a more
meaningful way to the vision you have for your
life as a whole. Your life will be amazingly
different when: You define what is supremely
important, keep that vision focused in your
mind, and take steps each day to walk in it —
doing things in concert with your core values.

Dale Galloway has stated, "People never
grow or go beyond their vision. Tell me your
vision and I will tell you your future."

Most people truly desire to be successful and
to have successful lives. Yet each one of us has
a different opinion of what success means.

**I believe the true definition of success is
fulfilling the purposes for which God has
created you.** It is accomplishing the dreams God
has had for you from before you were even born!

*"Dream lofty
dreams, and as
you dream, so shall
you become.
Your vision is the
promise of what
you shall one
day be."*
— James Allen

What is Your Definition of Success?

What is true success in your eyes? How will it look in your life? What do you really want to have happen? If you don't define what success *will* mean or *does* mean to you — then you will never know if you have achieved it. It is all too easy to be squeezed into someone else's "mold" of success. Consequently, you won't feel successful even if you attain many of the world's standards of success.

Some people are so paralyzed with the fear of failure that they basically just sit on the sidelines of life. In my mind, one of the worst things any person can do is to *waste their life by doing nothing*. It is better to move forward, and make mistakes than to look back and do nothing. It's not where you've been that's important, it's the direction in which you are going.

Whatever mistakes or failures you have had, God has given you the incredible power to **choose** to change. You can have a fresh new beginning in life every day. *Remember, it's the finish and not the start that counts.*

"Vision is of God! A vision comes in advance of any task well done."
— Katherine Logan

For What Purpose Were You Created?

* To live with low esteem? No!
* To be negative, fearful or defeated? No!
* To waste your potential? No!
* To live in poverty? No!

You were created to be successful, to fulfill your destiny, to bring happiness to the heart of God through both the ups and downs of life.

In this chapter, it is my desire to help you clearly define your vision and begin the process of writing it down and making it clear, so you can literally 'run with it' on a daily basis. The next chapter will assist you in clarifying your values and developing a personal mission statement. Later, you'll align your goals, plans, habits and behavior with your vision, values and mission. *This is a system that really works — when you apply it!*

What is Vision?

"*Success is not where you start, but where you finish.*"

Vision is the ability, or the God-given gift, to see those things which are not as though they were. To see things in your mind's eye *before* they exist. There is a strong correlation between vision and faith. Faith truly is the substance of things hoped for, the evidence of things unseen. Do we need faith if we can *already see* something? Faith is only required when we can't physically reach out and touch something. Faith is only needed when nothing else makes sense in the natural. In order to see clearly we need eyes of faith or 'faith-vision goggles' if you will!

One of Gutzon Borglum's great works as a sculptor is the head of Lincoln in the Capitol in Washington. He had cut it from a large square block of stone in his studio. One day, when the face of Lincoln was just becoming recognizable out of the stone, a young girl came by the studio with her parents. She looked at the half-done face of Lincoln, her eyes registering wonder and astonishment. She stared at the piece for a moment and then ran to the sculptor and asked, "Is that Abraham Lincoln?"

He replied, "Yes."

The little girl said, "Well, how in the world did you know that Mr. Lincoln was in that block of stone?"

In his book, "Seven Habits of Highly Effective People," Stephen Covey made popular the phrase, "beginning with the end in mind." This is based on the principle that everything has been created twice. The first creation is done in the imagination — in the mind, and the second is done in the physical realm where the first creation becomes tangible. When you begin with the end in mind, you start with a crystal clear picture — a vision — of your ultimate destination.

The creation of mankind is the ultimate illustration of this principle. In the beginning God decided to make mankind in his image — in his likeness. The 'first creation' started in the mind of God when this wonderful idea first came to him. He pictured in his infinite mind every detail of our creation, every intricacy of being made in his image *before he spoke the word* to bring mankind into physical existence.

God is the ultimate visionary! He visualized the entire creation, mankind, the earth and the rest of the universe before it was ever created. Visions and dreams come from him. He longs to envision you with his plans for your life. A great example of this is found in the book of Genesis when God gave a vision to Abraham. He took him outside and said, 'Look up at the heavens and count the stars — if indeed you can count them.' Then he said to him, 'So shall your offspring be,' and Abraham believed! God gave him a clear picture to help him visualize the end result of the vision. God can and will do the same for you and me if we are willing to ask him for it.

Ralph Waldo Emerson once said, "A believer is never disturbed because other persons do not yet see the fact which he sees."

Charles Goodyear was a believer, even though others could not yet see what he saw. At one point in his life, he had himself thrown into jail in order to gain time to reach his goals.

"With good vision, you not only see with your eyes but with your heart."
— Zig Ziglar

One of America's ten great industrial inventors, Goodyear was a failure for years. He owed money to friends, neighbors, and relatives who had backed him. He was penniless in 1838 when he discovered the method of vulcanizing rubber. However, by that time, with his invention still to be perfected, creditors had begun to hound him. Despite his repugnance to the idea, he fled to the protection of the bankruptcy laws. Soon afterward he was thrown into jail for contempt of court and there, unmolested behind prison bars, he perfected his rubber process. He not only paid off his creditors but made fortunes for all who had kept faith in him.

Do you know that God loves dreamers? It is the dreamer who brings about changes in our world and who finds the real satisfaction of living. Dreamers have explored the earth and have charted the heavens. They have been responsible for our greatest inventions. It is the dreamer who leaves the world a better place by challenging the status quo.

"God brings his vision to fulfillment not through our strength, but by his strength working in us."
— Randy Phillips

When we think of dreamers in the scriptures who first comes to mind? Joseph — the cocky seventeen year old, favorite son of Jacob. Although Joseph received his dreams from God, he sure needed a lesson on tactfulness when it came time to sharing them! Sometimes God wants us to keep dreams and visions to ourself and *let him* bring them to pass in due time.

Perhaps you're familiar with the story of how Joseph was sold into slavery by his brothers and ended up in Potiphar's house in Egypt. God blessed and prospered him, but then he was falsely accused of raping Potiphar's deceitful wife and wound up in prison. Once in prison, God again raised Joseph up to a position of leadership and influence. Finally, thirteen years after 'going down' to Egypt, God intervened in a major way.

God helped Joseph interpret Pharoah's dreams and he was brought out of prison and placed second in command over all of Egypt. In America today, this would be similar in magnitude to an illegal alien in prison on a rape sentence, coming straight out of prison and stepping into the Vice-Presidency — *in one day!* Are your circumstances impossible? So were Joseph's! God is able to do the impossible in your life.

"Life expects something of you, and it is up to every individual to discover what it should be."
— Victor Frankl

What does the book of Genesis record concerning Joseph's relationship with God? "He was with him and gave him success in everything he did." *May God grant the same for you and me!*

The other day I ran across the story of how a friend of another great dreamer missed quite an opportunity. One day, this friend was taken for a ride far out in the country. They drove off the main road and through groves of trees to a large uninhabited expanse of land. A few horses were grazing, and a couple of old shacks remained. Walter stopped the car, got out and started to describe with great vividness the wonderful things he was going to build. He wanted his friend Arthur to buy some of the land surrounding his project and get in on the ground floor. But Arthur thought to himself, "Who in the world is going to drive 25 miles for this crazy project? The logistics of the venture are staggering."

And so Walter explained to his friend Arthur, "I can handle the main project myself, although it will take all my money. But the land bordering it, where we're standing now, will in just a couple of years be jammed with hotels and restaurants and convention halls to accommodate the people who will come to spend their entire vacation here at my park." He continued, "I want you to have the first chance at this surrounding acreage, because in the next five years it will increase in value several hundred times."

"What could I say? I knew he was wrong," Arthur tells the story today. "I knew that he had let a dream get the best of his common sense, so I mumbled something about a tight-money situation and promised that I would look into the whole thing a little later on."

"Later on will be too late," Walter cautioned Arthur as they walked back to the car. "You'd better move on it right now."

And so Art Linkletter turned down the opportunity to buy up all the land that surrounded what was to become Disneyland. His friend, Walt Disney, tried to talk him into it. But Art thought he was crazy.

"If you can dream it, you can do it."
— Walt Disney

Why Do We Need a Vision?

Vision gives us direction, focus and stability. It is an energizing — motivating force in our lives! If I were to approach most people and ask them to show me where they have written down their vision, probably less than one in a hundred would be prepared to produce a vision statement. We need to get our vision written down!

In the book of Proverbs we read, "Where there is no vision, the people perish." Or, "Where there is no revelation, the people cast off restraint." The vision helps you to follow God's plan, much like guide rails are designed to keep you on a bridge, safe from falling headlong onto the rocks below.

Without an overriding sense of purpose and mission in life, what is worth living for? People are literally dying inside because they have no vision in their lives. Deep within all of us is the desire to make our lives and what we do with them count. There is nothing like an all consuming vision that will give you the purpose and meaning you long for.

With a vision, life is exciting! Every day becomes a new adventure. It's vision that will add enthusiasm and excitement to your life. Without a vision it's hard enough to survive, let alone thrive.

Casey Treat once said, "The way you *see* life is the way you will *live* your life. The way you *see* your future will be the way you *live* your future. If you *see* the potential, the possibilities and the exciting opportunities that are before you, then you will *experience* the blessings of that good vision. If you see dead-ends, impossibilities, and a victimized life with no opportunity then you will experience the consequences of that bad vision. If your vision is good, your life will be lit up with the blessings of God. If your vision is bad, your life will be darkened by the emptiness of the world."

"If you take the train off the tracks, it's free but it can't go anywhere."
— Anonymous

The proverb says, "He who seeks good finds good will, but evil comes to him who searches for it." In other words, "You get what you look for!"

Another word from Solomon says "Let your eyes look straight ahead, fix your gaze directly before you. Make level paths for your feet and take only ways that are firm. Do not swerve to the right or the left; keep your foot from evil." Kevin's unauthorized translation: "Have a vision for your life, keep it focused and directly in front of you. Prepare your surroundings and make it easy for you to follow the vision. Don't chase any hair-brained schemes, take no detours and beware of shortcuts!"

We Need to Know Where we are Going!

In the world today, there are many people who appear to be successful on the outside, but without God's vision in their lives, they are, in reality, getting nowhere fast. As the airplane pilot explained to the passengers, "Ladies and gentlemen, I have good news and bad news. The bad news is the plane's instrumentation has gone haywire and we don't know where in the world we're going. The good news is there is a tail wind behind us and we're making good time!"

Oliver Wendell Holmes, the eminent Supreme Court justice, was on a train reading his paper when the conductor came by punching tickets. The justice searched his coat pockets for his ticket. Then he searched his vest pocket. Each time he came up empty. Finally the conductor, who recognized him said, "Mr. Justice Holmes, don't worry. I'm sure the great Pennsylvania Railroad won't mind if you send your ticket to us when you find it." With this the distinguished jurist looked up at the conductor and said, "My dear young man — the problem is not where is my ticket? The problem is — where am I going?"

Even the brightest people can have a lack of vision and be short-sighted. Here are a few examples of poor vision from the past:

"What can be more palpably absurd than the prospect held out of locomotives traveling twice as fast as stagecoaches?"
— *The Quarterly Review, 1825*
"The ordinary 'horseless carriage' is at present a luxury for the wealthy; and although its price will probably fall in the

"Worse than being blind would be to be able to see but not have any vision."
— Helen Keller

"If you pursue two hares, both will escape you."
— Greek Proverb

near future, it will never, of course, come into as common use as the bicycle."
— *The Literary Digest, 1889*

"As a means of rapid transit, aerial navigation could not begin to compete with the railroad."
— *William Baxter, Jr. Popular Science, 1901*

"While television theoretically and technically may be feasible, commercially and financially, I consider it an impossibility, a development of which we need not waste time dreaming."
— *Lee Deforest, Scientist and Inventor, 1926*

"Folly delights a man who lacks judgment, but a man of understanding keeps a straight course."
— Proverbs

How Do You Get a Vision?

The first step to receiving your vision is to simply ask God to make it clear to you. Seek the Lord, spend time in prayer, for he knows the plans he has for you, and he longs to reveal them to you. Jeremiah the prophet tells us God has "Plans to prosper you and not to harm you, plans to give you hope and a future."

"But I was an accident," I hear some people say. "Does God still have a vision for me?" Absolutely! I know this is true personally, because I too could be labeled an "accident." My Mother became pregnant with me when she was only 15 and I'm so glad that abortion wasn't a strong option back in 1962 (not that Mom would have even seriously considered it). The pressure to 'take care of the situation' wasn't nearly the same as it is today and as a result, I have had the opportunity to live!

I take great comfort in the Psalm that so beautifully states (the Psalmist is speaking to God) "...your eyes saw my unformed body. All the days ordained for me were written in your book before one of them came to be."

Look Beyond the Present

The second key to defining your personal vision is to look beyond your present set of circumstances and fix your gaze into the future. A friend of mine once told me a story that perfectly illustrates this point. Joe Ellis grew up in a poor family. They tended a large garden to help put food on the table. Joe's dad loved to get the plow and carefully carve out rows as straight as a taut rope while his children planted seeds behind him. He was extremely particular with the accuracy of the furrows. One day Joe asked him, "Dad, can I try plowing the rows?"

"Why innovate? Because we're human. After all, we didn't stop at the wheel, did we? What does innovation take? Vision!"

His father turned to him and said, "You can sure give it a try, but remember it looks easier than you think to keep the rows straight." Joe was excited to get this opportunity so he took hold of that plow and fixed his gaze directly in front of his feet in order to keep the row straight. It didn't take long for Joe to look back at the row to see how he was doing. The row was crooked! It meandered this way and that way despite the careful attention he had given to the direction. "Dad, how can I make the rows as straight as you do?"

Joe's dad walked out to him and proceeded to tell him his secret, "Son, when I start a row I line up the plow with a fence post in the distance and I never take my eyes off it till each row is completed. I use it as a guidepost to keep me on track."

A vision should be just that, a guidepost that keeps us on track with God's plan for our lives. We do a poor job of staying on course if we only look in front of our feet, day by day. The key to reaching your goals is to look beyond the present, beyond where you are currently, and with the Lord's help, focus on the future vision of what *can be* in your life!

You know what happens when you fix your gaze directly in front of your feet? You're liable to bump into things. I speak from experience — *I've done it on at least three occasions!*

The funniest of these (at least in my wife's eyes) happened in London while on a Youth With A Mission (YWAM) outreach. Patty and I were engaged at the time and we enjoyed frequenting a local park for our after dinner walks. One blustery evening, the rain started pouring down in sheets so we decided to make a run for it back to the house where we were staying. We were running along, hand in hand, laughing and gazing into each other's eyes, only occasionally checking our bearings as to what lay before us.

"Great minds have purposes; others have wishes."
— Washington Irving

Now for some reason that I haven't quite figured out, the English have a bad habit of setting their light poles in from the street one third of the sidewalk's width. Needless to say, because I wasn't looking far enough ahead (actually looking sideways) I smacked right into one of those mean, eight-sided, washed aggregate concrete poles while running at a pretty good clip.

All of a sudden Patty looks over to see me bounce off the pole, catch my glasses in mid-air and end up flat on my back! Every part of my right side that came in contact with the pole was bruised or bleeding and guess what her reaction was? She started to laugh hysterically — I should have called off the engagement right then and there! I did indeed forgive her and we were married in El Paso, Texas on November 28, 1991. We have enjoyed almost 18 years of marriage together at the time of this writing — *and the best is yet to come!*

Guidelines for Your Vision:

As a believer in God, you will want your vision to be in alignment with these points:

1. In alignment with your faith.

God has had a plan for your life since the very beginning — make sure your vision is in alignment with it. Your faith should confirm your dreams and vision, not conflict with it.

"A vision is a guidepost that keeps you on track with God's plan for your life."
— Kevin Baerg

2. Must be balanced.

God is balanced and he desires us to live in balance. Your vision should take into consideration every aspect of your life without sacrificing one area for another. For example, God obviously doesn't want you to get so focused on your *vocation* that you forget about taking a *vacation* with your family!

3. Must be part of your heart — have a passion for it.

If your heart is not in something, I would question the Lord long and hard before pursuing it. If God wants you to do something big for him, I believe he'll give you a passion and a drive to see it through. This is not to say it'll be easy or that you'll have a continual excitement about it.

4. Must be concise, clear and simple — *yet exciting and compelling.*

The more complicated and unfocused your vision, the less apt you will be to stay on track and follow it through. The prophet tells us to make the vision simple (easy to grasp) and to 'inscribe it' or write it down!

How to Keep the Vision

1. **Write it down** and think about it often — read it out aloud daily.
2. **Thank God for it** and the privilege of following his vision for your life.
3. **Remember the vision** when you encounter obstacles and challenges — God gave it to you *before* the problems came!
4. **Imagine how many lives will be touched** by your vision, your life, and the relationships you develop along the way.

"Your word is a lamp to my feet and a light for my path."
— Psalms

You will find true success when you do what the proverb says. "In everything you do, put God first, and he will direct you and crown your efforts with success."

Your dreams won't necessarily come to you on a silver platter. Don't wait for the 'seventh wave of success' to carry you to the shore. Don't sit around waiting for your ship to come in if you haven't sent one out! Your destiny isn't automatic and you aren't on automatic pilot. You still fly your own 'jet' even though God knows your destination and every mile of your journey.

Perhaps, part of the problem is an improper belief system. It's hard to balance the truth that God is sovereign — what he says goes, and the seemingly opposite truth that man has been given complete responsibility for his decisions and behavior.

Somehow, I believe that God knows every choice you will make, but he doesn't choose for you. Your ultimate destiny is decided through the millions of daily choices you make over a lifetime. Yet God in his greatness already knows what you will choose.

We must not sit back, relax and think that

God's will is automatically done in our lives and in the world — *it isn't!* We can, however, get our plans and decisions in alignment with his best for us by taking time to ask God in prayer. With God as our strength, we can take responsibility for our actions and enjoy an exciting life of excellence.

Personal Application:

What is true success in your eyes? How will it look played out in your life? What do you really want to have happen? Writing this down is a powerful action step. When you write things down you are literally making a commitment.

Former Chairman and CEO of Chrysler Corporation, Lee Iaccoca stated it well, "What do you want to do? What do you want to be? What do you want to have? Where do you want to go? Who do you want to go with? How do you plan to get there? Write it down. Go do it. Enjoy it. Share it. It doesn't get much simpler or better than that."

Obviously this sort of thing could be several pages in length, but I'm asking you to capsulize your thoughts in a simple statement you can rally your life behind. Before you get started, I'd like to share my personal vision with you.

> *To be a source of inspiration and hope to all of God's people, challenging them to achieve excellence while actively pursuing God's purposes for their lives.*

So take the amount of time necessary — right this moment — and write out what you believe to be the vision and purpose for your life. Choose your words carefully, yet don't worry about perfection. You can always tune it up later. *Do it now!*

"Some people see things as they are and say, 'why?' I dream things that never were and say, 'why not?'"
— George Bernard Shaw

My Personal Vision

_____

"What you commit   _____
yourself to become,
determines what   _____
you are."
— Tony Campolo   _____

_____

_____

_____

_____

2 The Building Blocks of Character
— *Clarifying & Aligning Your Values*

"Your values and your character are wrapped up together. What you value and what you really are, is one and the same."
— *Clarence Jordan*

Who you are as a person — your character — is largely dependent on what you value in life. Values are the windows through which your decisions are made. Your character is determined by those decisions. In this chapter, you will learn how to clarify what is truly valuable to you. Not just what you *say* is valuable, but what you *give* value to through the expenditure of your time, money, energy and emotion. You will also develop a personal 'mission statement' for your life that will put energy and excitement into everything you do!

"Outstanding people have one thing in common: an absolute sense of mission."
— Zig Ziglar

A very wealthy man bought a huge ranch in Arizona, and he invited some of his closest associates over to see it. After touring some of the 1500 acres of mountains, rivers and grasslands, he took everybody to the house. The house was as spectacular as the scenery, and in the back was the largest swimming pool you have ever seen. However, this gigantic swimming pool was filled with alligators.

The rich owner explained it this way. "I value courage more than anything else. Courage is what made me a billionaire. In fact, I think that courage is such a powerful virtue that if anybody is courageous enough to jump in that pool, swim through those alligators and make it to the other side, I'll give them anything they want. Anything — my house, my land, even my money."

Of course, everybody laughed at the absurd challenge and proceeded to follow the owner into the house for lunch. Suddenly, they heard a splash. Turning around they saw a man swimming for his life across the pool, thrashing at the water, as the alligators swarmed behind him. After several death defying seconds, the man made it to the other side unharmed. The rich host was absolutely amazed, but he stuck to his promise.

He said, "You are indeed a man of courage and I will stand by my word. What do you want? You can have anything — my house, my land, my money — just tell me what you want and it is yours."

The swimmer, breathing heavily, looked up at the host and said, "I just want one thing — I want to know who pushed me in?!'"

What Do You Value More Than Anything?

"The harder the conflict, the more glorious the triumph. What we obtain too cheaply, we esteem too lightly; 'tis dearness only that gives every-thing its value."
— Thomas Paine

The rich host in the above story stated that he valued courage more than anything else. What can you make the same declaration about?

Identifying values will help you clarify what is truly important and where you should focus your energy and resources. In order to set personal goals that are worthwhile and vital to your mission, you first need to know **who you are** and **what you want out of life.** In simple terms, the question is, **where are you going** and **why are you going there?** The 'how' will become apparent once you have made the clear distinction concerning what you want. You can accomplish so much more if there is a big enough 'why' compelling you to go after it.

What is a Value?

Values are basically who or what is most important to you. You may value a relationship, a vocation, an experience, a character quality, an education, material goods, personal growth, recreation or just about anything.

Again, values are also the windows through which your decisions are made. In other words, when a choice between actions confronts us, we tend to choose the action that is consistent with our values. In response you might say, "If that's true then why do I find myself spending very little time with my family and yet my relationship with them is listed as one of my top values?"

My response is that there is obviously an incongruence between what you *say* you value and what you *actually* attach value to in the 'reality trenches' of daily living. **Saying you value something is meaningless unless you follow through with actions and decisions to support that value**. When you make decisions that *are consistent* with your uppermost values, the results are much more fulfilling and have a greater impact.

What Does God Value?

Throughout the scriptures we find out God values many things. Perhaps the biggest thing we discover is that God values character more than anything else. Qualities like:

- Compassion
- Kindness
- Humility
- Gentleness
- Patience

- Forgiveness
- Love

To name just a few.

We must not allow selfish values to infiltrate our lives and change our value system into one that God despises. Let's use Moses as an example, who by faith "when he had grown up, refused to be known as the son of Pharaoh's daughter. He chose to be mistreated along with the people of God rather than to enjoy the pleasures of sin for a short time."

The book of Micah tells us, "He has showed you, O man, what is good. And what does the Lord require of you? To act justly and to love mercy and to walk humbly with your God."

Of course the scriptures are chock full of other passages that share what God values in us. As people who believe in the Lord, we choose to value what God values and make sure our actions and behavior line up with those values.

"Character is what you are in the dark."
— Dwight L. Moody

How Do You Discover Your True Values?

1. **Go to the source** of all value — our loving Creator! Talk with him about *his values* and *your values.*
2. **Spend time reflecting** on the lives of those you admire. What values do they have that helped them to get where they are now?
3. **Think back** to when you were happiest to be alive (perhaps that is right now). What were you doing? Who were you with?

With our limited experiences how do we know something we might value more isn't just around the corner? The truth of the matter is...we don't! God wants to lead us and as we follow his plan, I believe he will put us in situations where *we can* discover our ultimate values. Sometimes we need to go out of our way to make these discoveries.

Such was the case with a young woman named Connie who rejected people and became a lonely individual. Reading, working, and taking care of her apartment became the focal interests in her life. Connie's whole life was changed when she began to send ten dollars a month to Helga — an adopted child overseas.

From a growing interest in Helga, Connie learned a fair amount of German, and made a trip to Hamburg to see her. Having become somewhat of an authority on Germany, the travel company which Connie worked for gave her a promotion. With the increase in her wages, she adopted another child, a little French boy. Finally, she adopted three additional children, two in Italy and one in Greece. She saw the lives of these five children blossom with her investment of time and finances. Connie had learned how to put the value of people above things. *Her values changed when she went beyond herself.*

When you start each day with your top values in mind, and challenges come, you can choose your response based on your values instead of reacting with emotion. You will be empowered to act in a proactive fashion with integrity, driven by your values instead of being cornered by your circumstances.

"If you insist on measuring yourself, put the tape around your heart rather than your head. Try measuring your wealth by who you are, rather than what you have."
— Carol Trabelle

Beginning with the Very End in Mind

To assist you in determining your values, please take a few moments to reflect on this 'picture' in your mind:

You are present at your own memorial service. Many people have come to pay their respect and honor you and your family with their love and appreciation for your life. You look at the program and notice there are to be four speakers. The first is from your immediate family (although your extended family is also there). The second to speak is your closest friend. The third is a colleague from work and the fourth is the minister.

Take the time to think in depth. What would you like each one of these people to say about you and the life you lived? What kind of spouse, parent or child would be described by their words? What kind of friend or co-worker? What character traits would you like them to mention having seen in your life? What accomplishments would you want to be remembered for? As you look in your mind's eye at those around you, what impact would you like to have made in their lives?

"Be driven by your values, not cornered by your circumstances."
— Kevin Baerg

Personal Application:

1. Write down some of the reflections from your 'memorial service':

   _____

   _____

   _____

   _____

   _____

2. What do you truly value in life? List your values, in any order, as they come to mind. Don't make any distinctions on whether your life is currently in alignment with them or not.

   _____

   _____

_____

_____

_____

_____

_____

_____

_____

3. Select the top five values from your list
and place them in order of priority.

1. Honesty

2. Integrity

3. Kindness

4. Trustworthy

5. _____

*"You gotta be
before you can do.
You gotta do before
you can have."*
— Zig Ziglar

4. Now for the painful part! Is your life
currently in alignment with your top five
values? If someone were to live with you
for one month and evaluate how you
spent your time and money, what would
their list of *your* top five values be? Take a
few moments and be brutally honest with
yourself. List your five 'current reality
values.' Prioritize them based on how
much time and resources you have
allocated to them in the past year.

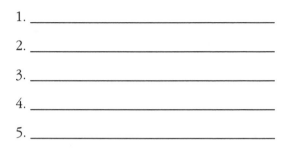

5. How different are your two lists? What actions can you take to bring these lists in alignment with each other? This is what congruency and integrity are all about: **Being on the inside what we say we are on the outside.**

Personal Mission Statement

In the first chapter I shared with you the principle of beginning with the end in mind. One of the most effective ways to accomplish this is by creating your own personal mission statement. This statement should concentrate on your **character** — who you want to become, as well as your **accomplishments** — what you want to do. You also want to include the values that are foundational to 'becoming' and 'doing.' Remember, the 'doing' follows the 'becoming.' "We are human becomings, not human doings."

Stephen Covey states that, "another way to understand a personal mission statement is to approach it as your personal constitution." The constitution of the United States of America is the foundation for its entire system of justice. There have only been twenty-six amendments to the constitution in over two hundred years and ten of them were in the original Bill of Rights. It is the written standard for this great nation and is virtually changeless at its core. A personal mission statement that is based on godly values can become a similar standard for an individual. It becomes your personal constitution and, as such, is the foundation for decision-making.

People find it hard to live with change when they don't have a changeless core inside them. Growing through change is much easier when an individual has a changeless view of who they are, what they value and where they are going. Your written personal mission statement is the scale upon which every life decision, such as productively using your time, talents and treasure, can be weighed.

As you take the time to actually sit down and work it out you will feel, as Covey aptly states, "a great sense of clarity, commitment, freedom and exhilaration!" It will change you because it will cause you to do some deep thinking about your priorities and challenge you to align your actions with your beliefs. You won't be buffeted by the winds of change and everything that is happening around you. *You will have a wonderful sense of mission in your life!*

"A mission could be defined as an image of a desired state that you want to get to. Once fully seen, it will inspire you to act, fuel your motivation and determine your behavior."
— Charles Garfield

Your Life Roles

One way to make your mission statement easier to develop is to break it down into the specific roles you play in life and the long-range goals you have for each one. Think about your personal roles, such as a child of God, a spouse, parent and friend. Consider your professional roles on the job or in your career. What do you want to *become* and *do* in these areas?

Working out your mission in light of the vital roles in your life helps ensure balance and peace. Taking the opportunity to frequently review your roles will prompt you to not get so involved in one area that you neglect other roles that may even more important to you.

Some people get so wrapped up in their work that their health suffers. Others are so driven toward 'success' that they leave their family and friends in the dust. Still others are overly committed to recreation and having a good time, leaving them few opportunities to accomplish anything of significance.

Once you have identified your roles, think about the long-term results you want to have in each of these areas. Since these goals are an extension of your vision, values and mission, they will be very different from the type of goals most people usually set. Your goals belong to you. They are not for someone else — they are yours! They will be a mirror-image of your strongest values, your unique gifts and calling as well as your mission in life.

"God wants us to be balanced, to live our lives in the 'radical middle!'"
— John Dawson

Remember, an effective goal is more concerned with results than activity. It directs you to where you want to be and, by deduction, reveals where you are. It will give you the necessary information to reach your destination and let you know when you get there. And when your goal is broken down into daily actions you will enter the 'proactive zone' where, with God's help, you take charge of your life, making things happen to fulfill your purpose.

Identifying your roles and goals helps you to create and put order in your personal mission statement. Clearly defining the different areas of your life and deciding what two or three long-range outcomes or results you desire in each of them will provide you with a tremendous sense of direction and perspective.

When we move into chapter nine, we'll go

into greater detail with short and mid-range goals. The important step right now is to identify your roles and the long-range goals within them as they relate to your personal mission statement.

Personal Application:

1. List your roles in life. For example: Child of God, spouse, parent, friend, teacher (job/career), volunteer, coach (community service). What long-term results do you want to have in each of these areas? List two or three outcomes under each one.

1. Role: _Daughter_

Results: • _Serve_ _LOVE_
• _Honor_ _Parents_
• _Make Proud_

2. Role: _Upline / Downline_

Results: • _Create Relationships_
• _Serve_ • _Touch Lives_
• _LOVE PPL_

3. Role: _Friend_

Results: _Always there_
Encourage

4. Role: _Child of God_

Results: • _Grow the Kingdom_
• _Live at Peace_
• _Live Abdnantly_

5. Role: _Volunteer_

Results: _Serve_

___

Not Impactful

6. Role: _Engraver_

Results: _Make memories_

Passive Income

___

"To love what you do and feel that it matters — how could anything be more fun?"
— Katherine Graham

7. Role: _Impactor_

Results: _- Use my god giver abilities to impact people's lives._

2. Review your list of values and weave them together with your roles and results into an exciting personal mission statement. For some examples of personal mission statements, please see page 187.

My Mission Statement –

___

___

___

___

___

___

_____
_____
_____
_____
_____

*"Ability with-
out honor has
no value."*
— Ralph Waldo Emerson

_____
_____
_____

*Good-
powerful*

_____
_____
_____
_____
_____
_____
_____
_____
_____
_____
_____

_____

_____

_____

_____

_____

_____

"God did not create   _____
you to live life on
the sidelines, but to   _____
win the game!"
—Dale Galloway   _____

_____

3 Breaking Glass Ceilings
— *Identifying and Changing Your Limiting Beliefs*

"I can do everything through God who gives me strength."

— *St. Paul*

Everyone has experienced the damaging effect of living with limitations. Limitations we impose upon ourselves or limitations others have placed on us. This chapter will help you discover what some of these 'glass ceilings' are in your life and how to smash through them into new levels of growth and accomplishment!

"It's not who you are that holds you back, it's who you think you're not."
— Bob Moawad

A young man tells this story about limitations:

"One summer as I was packing to spend three months with relatives at the lake up north, my dad asked me to take my goldfish with me, because he didn't want to take care of it all summer.

The day after we got up to the lake, I decided to become a liberator. I went down to the dock with my fish bowl and gave my fish a little talk. 'I'm going to throw you in this lake,' I said. 'You will be free. You can eat well here and grow up to be a big fish.' When I put the goldfish in the water at the end of the dock, it stayed right there. I backed off, thinking the fish was attached to my shadow. But when I moved back to be sure it was gone, it was still right there. I even threw a stone into the water to scare it away, but that goldfish just swam around it.

When I came back after lunch, the goldfish was still there, swimming in the same spot. I sat down and thought, 'That fish should be free.

It's got the whole lake to swim in.' Suddenly I saw in the water a huge ripple. Splash! A big bass swallowed my little goldfish.

Later in life someone told me that a goldfish, once it has lived in a circumference of a certain size, **has been conditioned to think small.** It will stay there until it dies — swimming around in that small circle."

What size of fish bowl or container are you conditioned to live in? How did you get conditioned that way? How much potential did the goldfish have? *How much potential do you have?*

"Your past is not your potential. In any hour you can choose to liberate the future."
— Marilyn Ferguson

Exponential Potential

Let's take a look at your potential. Potential can be likened to an iceberg. The majority of the mass of an iceberg (8/9) is found below the surface of the water. Only 1/9 of the bulk of the iceberg can be seen. Your potential can be compared to the whole iceberg and your effectiveness (what you use of your potential) is just the tip above the water. Scientists estimate we use less than 10% of the most awesome computer known to mankind — our brain. The purpose of this book is to give you tools to turn much more of your potential into effective living.

There are many different areas of potential in life. Here are six major categories:

1. Spiritual/Personal Growth _____

2. Relational (Family & Friends) _____

3. Vocational _____

4. Financial/Material _____

5. Recreational _____

6. Physical/Health _____

Personal Application

How much of your potential do you estimate you are reaching in these areas? Put a percentage in the space provided by each one. Do you have a 'lop-sided wheel?' Are there areas you need to work on to bring about a better balance in your life?

Four ingredients of Potential

1. **God-given Ability/Talent**
2. **Knowledge/Education/Training**
3. **Desire/Motivation**
4. **Attitudes/Self-Image**

Most people realize the first three ingredients are necessary to tap into the fullness of what we can become. Actually, it's the last ingredient that is most vital to bringing about the meaningful and lasting change one needs to experience in order to reach their full potential.

1. God-given Ability/Talent

Each one of us has been skillfully knit together in our mother's womb where God has bestowed gifts, abilities and talents before we were even born. We are all capable of doing so many things! I believe that God has also given each person unique talents to bless the rest of the world. You've probably heard it said before, "Talent is God's gift to you. What you do with it is your gift to God!"

All too often though, an extremely negative word crops up in most vocabularies by the time we reach junior high school. Some describe this as the ugliest four letter word. The word is 'can't.' I believe that we all have the ability to learn or accomplish whatever we choose or need to do.

Let me ask you a question. Can you speak Japanese? Most people say they can't. Are you aware that there are millions of children under the age of 10 in Japan that have no problem speaking Japanese! Did I ask you if you currently knew how to speak Japanese or even had a desire to learn? No! I just asked if you had the *ability* to do so.

What response would I get if I asked the same question to a group of five year olds? If there were 28 of them in the kindergarten class, how many hands do you think would go up? Twenty-eight? No — *fifty-six!* How would they put up their hands? They would throw both of them up in the air and shout out, "I can do it, I can do it!" Let me test you again. **Can** you speak Japanese? The key word is *can.*

Have you heard the story about the boy who wanted to march in the circus parade? When the show came to town, the bandmaster needed a trombonist, so the boy signed up. He hadn't marched a block before the fearful noises from his horn caused two women to faint and a horse to run away. The bandmaster demanded, 'Why didn't you tell me you couldn't play the trombone?'

Argue for your limitations and, sure enough, they're yours.
— Richard Bach

The boy replied, 'How did I know? I never tried before!'

Lest you start thinking, "this is all well and good for other people but I have too much going against me to ever succeed," consider these examples of overcoming adversity.

He didn't talk until he was four years old or read until he was seven. One of his teachers labeled him as "mentally slow, unsociable and adrift forever in his foolish dreams." His name: Albert Einstein.

"He possesses minimal football knowledge.

Lacks motivation." A so-called expert once said of Vince Lombardi.

Beethoven apparently liked to do his own thing and didn't spend much time learning the correct technique with his violin. His teacher said that Ludwig was hopeless as a composer.

Before he created Disneyland, Walt Disney went bankrupt several times. He was once fired by the editor of a newspaper for an apparent lack of ideas.

"He is too stupid to learn anything!" Declared Thomas Edison's 'perceptive' teachers.

Henry Ford failed miserably and went broke five times before finally succeeding with the automobile.

Babe Ruth, one of the all-time legends of Baseball, holds second place on the career home run list but is also second on a much less glorious list: Career strikeouts.

One of the greatest 'movers and shakers' of this century, made his most significant contributions as a 'senior citizen.' Winston Churchill was 62 before he finally became Prime Minister of England following a lifetime of setback and defeat, including failing the sixth grade.

Ingredient number one of potential is our God-given ability or talent and the good news is — *we all have it.* If there's a difference between where you currently are and where you would like to be, it's not any lack of ability, it is your attitude and the image of who you think you are or who think you're *not.*

2. Knowledge/Education/Training

There is a knowledge explosion occurring right now that is greater than ever before. In order to keep up with this torrid pace, you and I are challenged to continually be adding to our personal knowledge base. The book of Proverbs tells us that a wise person "stores up knowledge." An important point to remember is that *it isn't what you know*, it's *what you **do** with what you know*. You must apply your knowledge or it is useless to you. In light of this, how many of you (including me) know more about organization and time management than the current status of your desk would normally indicate? How many of you know more about physical fitness and proper nutrition than your current state of health and the content of your refrigerator would reveal? You know what most of us are? Educated derelicts! We don't even *use* what we *know*. The point I'm attempting to get across here is that in most cases we already **have** the knowledge to reach more of our potential. It's the 'putting it into practice' mode that we're working on.

3. Desire/Motivation

Some people would call me a motivational speaker or author, and that is true to a point. However, most people are already motivated to improve their lot in life. Let's quickly check your motivation. Have you ever had the desire to enjoy better communication with your spouse or your immediate family? How about wanting to better develop your relationship with God? Have you even once been motivated to better organize your time, your life, your desk and your trunk? See, you do have the desire — *you are motivated!*

Do you remember the last time you attempted to drive your car with the emergency brake fully engaged? You try to back up and you wonder why your car isn't moving like it should. So what do you do? Step on the gas until you get going, right? Some people have done it so often that it makes no difference anymore!

That's the way many of us attempt to change. Our parking brake is fully engaged, so we just press harder on the accelerator. "I'm going to change if it kills me!" And it just might. Wouldn't it make better sense to release the brake?

4. Attitudes/Self-Image

The fourth ingredient of potential is the real key to 'releasing the brake' on what you can achieve. This is one of the major areas you can work on that will have a tremendously profound affect on our your life.

It is impossible to perform consistently in a manner *inconsistent* with the way in which you see yourself in your 'mind's eye'. If you see yourself as an unhappy person, you'll be unhappy. If you see yourself as someone out of shape, you'll continually find yourself out of shape. Conversely, if your attitude is such that you see yourself as an athlete in great condition, you'll tend to find yourself at an excellent level of fitness. Truly, your attitude and the image you hold of yourself is the key that unlocks the door to your potential.

"To build a healthy self-image, finish the job."

Now that I've hopefully whet your appetite, we'll wait to learn more about attitudes and self-image in chapters six and seven.

Doing the Impossible

Remember how it was thought to be 'physically impossible' to run a mile in under 4 minutes? That was, of course, until Roger Bannister broke the 4 minute barrier in 1954. After he broke it, several other runners ran sub 4 minute miles the same year. The next year many more broke it. Now they're running miles in about 3 minutes and 44 seconds!

Speaking of running, I've got to tell you one of my favorite stories: Back around 1983, a 'young' man in his early sixties, Cliff Young from Australia, became a local hero. You see, Cliff loved to run — he'd run all his life. Since he didn't have a motorized vehicle, he ran all over his cattle ranch in the Australian outback.

Someone found out about his penchant for running and urged him to enter a 'fun run' from Melbourne to Sydney. For a quick geography refresher — that's a little over six hundred miles! Does that sound like a 'fun run' to you?

Well, Cliff decided to enter the event, but when he showed up at the starting line they thought he was a joke entrant. He was wearing his muck boots and bib overalls with a plastic water bottle and a little tube stuffed with raw beans, carrots and pumpkin. Of course, everyone else had on their ultralight running gear, the latest technological shoes, plus all the concentrated proteins, energy bars and juices. They knew what they were doing!

Cliff wasn't fazed by any of this. He just went out, ran his race and beat them **all** — *by a day!* How did he beat them by a day you ask? Everyone else believed they had to sleep at least six hours per day in order to cover the great distance. Totally unaware of their belief, Cliff averaged less than two hours of sleep per day and won the race by just around twenty-four hours! Would you take a guess at what happened the very next year? *Everybody* ran twenty-four hours faster. Why? Cliff had shattered the old 'belief', the previous glass ceiling, and had created a new reality in people's minds.

Do you want to know the rest of the story?

"Never tell a person that something cannot be done. God may have waited centuries for someone ignorant enough of the impossible to do that very thing."
— Dr. J.R. Holmes

He didn't realize there was a prize of ten thousand dollars for the winner, so he distributed it evenly among all the finishers. He also went on to marry a 21 year old young lady. A fellow Australian declared, "If that race didn't test his endurance, this surely will!"

Cliff became an instant celebrity — a legend in the 'land of wonder, the land down under!'

Nothing is Impossible with God

You'll never outgrow the limits you place on yourself, but you have the God-given power to raise or lower them. It's up to you. Remember, nothing is impossible with God!

In the year 1870 the Methodists in Indiana were having their annual conference. At one point, the president of the college where they were meeting said, "I think we live in a very exciting age."

The presiding bishop said "What do you see?"

The college president responded, "I believe we are coming into a time of great inventions. I believe, for example, that men will fly through the air like birds."

The bishop said, "This is heresy! The Bible says that flight is reserved for the angels. We will have no such talk here."

After the conference, the bishop, whose name was Wright, went home to his two small sons, Wilbur and Orville.

Well, you know the rest of the story and what the Wright brothers did to radically change their father's limiting belief!

Do you want to be known as a 'no-limit person?' Someone who does not let the limitations that most people accept get in their way.

I want to be like the bumblebee.   .
Aerodynamically, the bumblebee should be

"The Wright Brothers flew right through the smoke screen of impossibility."
— Charles F. Kettering

unable to fly. The size, weight and shape of its body in relation to its total wing span makes flying scientifically impossible. However, the bumblebee, being unschooled in scientific theory, goes ahead and flies anyway!

The Power of Conditioning

Years ago the Denver Zoo had a difficult decision to make. They were offered the gift of a beautiful, large polar bear, but the problem was that there was no existing space for it. At the time of the gift, the Board of Directors were in the middle of a fund-raising campaign to renovate the zoo. In their renovation plans, they changed the strategy to include a magnificent habitat for the polar bear. In the meantime, the bear was put in a small, temporary cage. The space was so small that it could only take three steps, turn around and walk three steps back.

Because of unforeseen delays the construction took three years, but its new home was indeed grand: waterfalls, caves and plenty of space to move around. The bear entered its new home, looked around, took three steps, turned around, and took three steps back, turned around, took three steps...

This is a parable of human life. Granted, we're more intelligent than animals, but we're just as apt to be conditioned. The trouble is we are so easily led to believe that we *can't* achieve something, we *can't* do this or we *can't* do that. Have you ever had anyone try and talk you out of your dreams?

"Nobody in our family has ever gone to college and you expect to go to Harvard? You're crazy!"

"What makes you think someone will hire you for that position? It'll be a snowy day in

Use the word 'impossible' with the greatest caution."
— Werner von Braun

summer before that happens!"

"You might as well forget your ambition to be a teacher, who wants to listen to you?"

"You think you can become an administrator? You can't even keep your desk organized!"

We all have the promise that life contains infinite possibilities, a vast environment to explore. Yet most of us settle for a routine that narrows our life to the dimensions of a prison cell. What have you settled for? What have you been conditioned to accept as your portion in life?

Personal Application:

What are some things you believe you 'can't' do? What are some of the limits you or others have placed on yourself? How have you been conditioned? Please jot down every limit that comes to your mind. When you do this, reflect on each of the six areas of potential: Spiritual, relational, vocational, financial, recreational and physical.

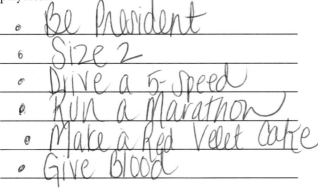

- Be President
- Size 2
- Drive a 5-speed
- Run a Marathon
- Make a Red Velet Cake
- Give Blood

_____

_____

_____

_____

_____

_____

_____

*"If we did all the
things we are
capable of, we
would literally
astound ourselves."*
— Thomas Edison

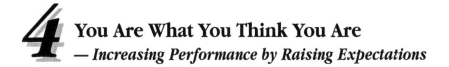

4 You Are What You Think You Are
— Increasing Performance by Raising Expectations

"For as he thinks within himself,
so he is."
— *Proverbs*

Your thinking determines the level of success you will achieve in any endeavor. In order to reach your full potential, you must have a firm understanding of how God wants you to think and the way in which your thought process works. This will facilitate you in changing from the inside out.

"All meaningful and lasting change starts on the inside and works its way out."
— Bob Moawad

The Power of Thought

Your mind is one of the most incredible creations of God. With it, you have been given the amazing ability to think. You have also been given the power to weigh your thoughts and finally to *choose* which ones you will focus on. Whether you focus on and cultivate positive thoughts or negative thoughts, the choice is totally up to you.

Let's look at a great story in the book of Numbers about Caleb and Joshua spying out the 'promised land.' Note Caleb's unbridled enthusiasm, "We should go up and take possession of the land, for we can certainly do it." He was full of faith and had a clear vision of what the Lord was able to do through the children of Israel. Yet even with this exhortation, the other spies went on to share their bad report. They saw giants in the land, men of great stature, and this is how they thought: "We seemed like grasshoppers in our *own* eyes, and we looked the same to them."

*"As I think—
I am, therefore if
I want to change
who I am, I must
first change the
way I think."*

They let their weak, natural minds control their thoughts and therefore their actions! One of the most famous proverbs states **"For as he thinks within himself, so he is."** This can be literally translated "as a man reckons in his soul, so he is." It's how you think down deep inside of you. There is no doubt that this is one of the defining scriptures when it comes to understanding the power of your thought life. It is interesting to note how accurate this proverb is in light of the ten spy's negative confession. They saw themselves as grasshoppers and therefore assumed that the giants saw them that way as well. Had they gone into battle, they would have fought like grasshoppers!

Ironically, we are told that the hearts of the former inhabitants of the promised land were actually *melting with fear* on account of Israel, because news of what transpired in Egypt (the plagues and the parting of the Red Sea) had already reached them!

How you perceive yourself is very important in life. **In fact, you will never be something you think you're not.** If you don't see yourself as someone who is strong in faith, you won't become a faith filled person. If you don't see yourself as a good communicator in your relationships, don't expect to have great communication with those close to you. **Rarely do we exceed our own expectations or perform at a level inconsistent with the picture we have of ourselves.**

Christian Herter was running hard for re-election as Governor of Massachusetts. One day he arrived late at a barbecue. He'd had no breakfast or lunch, and he was famished. As he moved down the serving line, he held out his plate and received one piece of chicken. The

Governor said to the serving lady, "Excuse me, do you mind if I get another piece of chicken. I'm very hungry."

The woman replied, "Sorry, I'm only supposed to give one piece to each person."

He repeated, "But I'm starved."

Again she stated, "Only one to a customer."

Herter was normally a modest man, but he decided this was the time to use the weight of his office, so he said, "Madam, do you know who I am? I am the governor of this state."

She answered, "Do you know who I am? I'm the lady in charge of the chicken. Move along, mister!" She obviously had a clear idea of who she was!

> *If you think you are beaten, you are;*
> *If you think you dare not, you don't;*
> *If you like to win, but think you can't*
> *It is almost certain you won't!*
> *If you think you'll lose, you're lost,*
> *For out in the world we find*
> *Success begins with a fellow's will;*
> *It's all in the state of mind.*
> *If you think you're outclassed, you are.*
> *You've got to think high to rise.*
> *You've got to be sure of yourself before*
> *You can ever win a prize.*
> *Life's battles don't go*
> *To the stronger or faster man,*
> *But sooner or later the man who wins*
> *Is the man who thinks he can!*
> — *Anonymous*

I first heard this poem on a cassette series my Dad bought back in my teens. It spoke to me then, it still speaks to me now!

In the last chapter you just finished an exercise where you listed some of your limiting beliefs — things you think you can't do that also might be holding you back. Some of these limiting beliefs or habits have been with you for some time, haven't they? How do you change a habit or change your way of thinking when you've been doing it for a long time? Let's say for example that you have the habit of being late for events since you were twelve and you're now 39. So, for 27 years you've been a tardy individual? On the one hand, the answer is yes. But on the other hand, you learned the habit in your twelfth year and have just repeated that habit 27 times. Isn't that an easier way to look at it? **Remember a habit is just a choice that has gained momentum.** To change the habit requires allowing the *right* choice to build momentum in your life.

"Years may wrinkle the skin, but to give up interest wrinkles the soul. You are as young as your faith, as old as your doubt; as young as your self-confidence, as old as your fear; as young as your hope, as old as your despair."

Let's use handwriting as another example. How long have you been handwriting? Since most people learn how to write when they're around five, take your age minus five for the answer. Now take a look at your handwritten answers to the questions at the end of the last chapter. You mean to tell me that you've been practicing that stuff for 24 years? Just look at the mess in front of you! You haven't practiced for 24 years, you learned how to do it once and then just wrote the way you first learned twenty-four consecutive years. It's the same thing with attitudes and beliefs. Once they are developed, you tend to repeat them and *keep acting like the person you think you are.*

How Does Your Thought Process Work?

There are three separate components that make up your thought process:

1. The Conscious Process

This is the process you are currently using to absorb the information from this book. You take in and process the data around you through your five senses, (sight, sound, touch, taste, and smell) associating and evaluating it with the data previously entered in your brain. Only information that is currently valuable to you makes it through the filters in your brain. The conscious process is best likened to a judge that helps you decide your course of action or inaction.

2. The Subconscious Process

This part of the thought process can be likened to a computer. It is impartial and unbiased and its operating system is the currently perceived 'truth and reality' of your life. It records and stores this perceived reality and takes care of automatic activities and habits.

Your Built-in Data Filtering System

Part of the subconscious mind is your own built-in data filtering system. Data comes in through your conscious mind via your senses and is run through your filter system. This part of your brain is designed to filter through the several million stimuli per second you are bombarded with and allow only profitable data to register in your conscious mind.

Basically, it decides what you will take notice of and give your attention to. It is your mind's screening process. Keep in mind that your conscious brain can only focus on a limited number of stimuli at any given moment. Therefore, your brain works hard to determine what *not* to give its attention to. As countless pieces of information zing your way each moment, your brain wades through most of it and focuses only on what is important to you at that time. The mechanism for making this happen is your built-in data filter. It is ultimately responsible for controlling how much perceived reality you *consciously* experience.

Let me show you how this works: Have you ever purchased or desired a new car and all of a sudden you see that model everywhere you go? Why did that occur? Was that model around before? Of course it was, but noticing it wasn't important to you and so your filter system didn't allow the data to get through. Now your filter system knows that anything related to a Ford Explorer for example, is important to you and should be recognized by your conscious mind. Immediately you have a highly increased awareness of something that has in reality been around you for some time.

When asked which one of his works he would pick as his greatest master-piece, architect Frank Lloyd Wright, at the tender age of 83, retorted, "My next one."

This shift in your thought process is designed by God to align your thinking with your goals. **Once you have made the decision that something is extremely important to you, any information that will help you achieve that goal will become clear.** This is further enhanced as you focus over and over on accomplishing it and allowing your emotions to get intensely involved. It's not critical to understand all the 'hows' of achieving a goal when you first set it. Know that your filter system will help collect all the data required as you head down the path toward your goal.

Let's test this out: If have a watch on, please take it off for a moment and put it face down before you. I want you to imagine you're at the local police station reporting a burglary in your home and the only thing taken was your watch. You now have 20 seconds to write down a description of the stolen watch on a police report. Please jot down in the space provided everything you can remember about your watch. Note the brand, color, special markings, etcetera. Does it have a second hand? What color is the face? Is it digital or analog? Write down everything you can, but be quick — the police department doesn't have all day!

Personal Application:

Police Report on Stolen Property

_____

_____

_____

_____

_____

Time's up! Now turn your watch over. Let me introduce you to your watch! Would you have some difficulty getting your watch back with the description you just wrote down? Do you notice any discrepancies? Did you possibly have the wrong brand name written down or forget you have a calendar? Did you think you have numbers, but in reality the face only has marks?

Please quickly turn it over once again. Now, can you tell me what the current time is?

What do you mean you don't know what time it is? You just looked at your watch!

What was your goal when you first looked at your watch? Normally the only thing that has value to you when you glance at your watch is the time. You don't need numbers or even all the slash marks. When you first turned your watch back over you were looking at it descriptively.

Perhaps you were saying to yourself, "I can't believe it, I didn't even put the right brand down, I put Rolex instead of Timex!" (a small error of five or six thousand dollars!) "I thought I had Roman numerals but they're just normal numbers. I can't believe I missed these things. What's that Kevin? The time? I have no idea — I was busy checking out the parts!"

See how the goals were different? It is amazing the amount of information you don't notice because you're not looking for it — you don't have a goal. **What information are you missing out on due to a lack of goals in your life?**

3. The Creative Subconscious Process

A 'controller' is the best representation of the creative subconscious. It gives you the motivation to attain your perceived truth and reality, whether it is the best thing for you or not. The creative subconscious' purpose is to resolve conflict, reduce tension, and solve problems creatively, all the while making sure that you act like **you**. It maintains your vision of yourself. If you picture yourself in a negative fashion, your creative subconscious will work to keep your performance equal to the current image that you hold. The power of the creative subconscious is really apparent when it becomes time to change.

Do you like to bowl? How much would your score normally be for one game? What happens when all of a sudden you get three strikes and a spare in the first 5 frames with over 100 points and you know you're normally a 150 bowler? What kind of thoughts enter into your mind? "I can't believe I'm bowling this good! This isn't like me to nail down a turkey (three strikes in a row). I don't think I can keep this up!"

Have you ever thought similar thoughts? How many times do you 'correct for the error' on the last 5 frames by going without a single strike or spare and manage just around 50 points and thus wallow in your '150' comfort zone? That is your creative subconscious at work making sure that you live up (or down) in accordance with who you think you are.

An old farmer had a mule that didn't know his own strength. As the farmer hitched up the mule to a two-horse plow, he would say, "Get up, Will. Get up, Kate. Get up, John. Get up, Betty Lou!"

A neighbor, hearing the farmer one morning, stopped and asked, "How many names does that mule have?"

"Oh, he has just one," replied the farmer. "His name is Pete. But I put blinders on him and call out all the other names so he will think other mules are helping him. That way, he does the work of at least two."

"The things that are foremost in our minds determine our actions and decisions. We become like our dominant thoughts."

How Does God Want Us to Think?

The book of Romans tells us "Do not think of yourself more highly than you ought, but rather think of yourself with sober judgment, in accordance with the measure of faith God has given you."

Does it say, "Think of yourself as a worm in the hands of an angry God"? No, God wants our thinking to be balanced, using "sober judgement" — yet without conceit.

Romans goes on to urge that we *be transformed by the renewing of our mind.* It is then we will be able to test and know what God's will for our lives truly is.

What Does God Want Us to Think About?

The book of Philippians states, "Finally, brothers, whatever is true, whatever is noble, whatever is right, whatever is pure, whatever is lovely, whatever is admirable — if anything is excellent or praiseworthy — think about these things."

This is one of my favorite verses and for good reason: It clearly delineates the kinds of thoughts we are to entertain. If what you spend the majority of your time thinking about doesn't fall within these parameters, you need to change. The reason God gives such explicit instructions concerning our thoughts is simple: **What we dwell upon, we become like**. What we think about, we eventually act on. I'm convinced that if a person properly applied this single verse, it would transform their life and the lives of those around them!

Personal Application:

In the last chapter I asked you to write down some things you believe you 'can't' do plus some of the limits you or others have placed on you. In closing, I want you to take that list and turn the negatives into positives. For example if you put down, "I always procrastinate," the positive opposite would be, "I take action." If you listed, "I'm a slow learner," change it to "I'm a quick study." Perhaps you wrote down, "I can't learn a second language." Translate that into "I find it easy learning a second language." Don't worry about the 'truthfulness' of everything just yet, we'll get into that later.

Take a couple of minutes now to identify positive opposites for the limiting beliefs, habits and attitudes that get in your way. You may

"If you want to be enthusiastic, act enthusiastic."
— Dale Carnegie

wish to refer to your notes at the end of the
third chapter.

Limitation — Positive Opposite

_____

_____

_____

_____

_____

_____

_____

_____

*"Believe it! High
expectations are
the key to
everything."*
— Sam Walton

"How we think determines how we feel. We can change the way we feel by changing our thinking. It's your thought life rather than your situation that determines your happiness."

5 The Awesome Power of Your Tongue
— *Speaking Words of Life.*

"The tongue has the power of life and death, and those who love it will eat its fruit."

— *Proverbs*

Not only does the tongue have the power of life and death in how you talk to others, but also in relation to how you talk to *yourself*. In this chapter you will learn how to use words to edify and empower anyone — *especially you!* You'll also look into how words trigger pictures that bring on emotions. This is one of the key areas that will help you become the incredible person you are capable of becoming.

A story is told of a master who told his servant to buy some good food. The servant returned with some tongue. Then the master asked the servant to purchase some bad food. Again, the servant returned with some tongue.

When the master pressed him for an explanation, the servant replied, "The tongue is both good and bad, when it is good, it is very good, but when it is bad, nothing is worse."

Your words can either hold you back or usher you into success. If you are not moving forward in victory and want to turn your life around, you need to change the words you use.

"Words are both better and worse than thoughts; they express them, and add to them; they give them power for good or evil; they start them on an endless flight, for instruction and comfort and blessing, or for injury, sorrow and ruin.
— Tyron Edwards

The Power of Words

Words are so potent that the entire universe was created using words. The book of Genesis states "and God said, 'Let there be light," and there was light." Three awesome words of creation; "and God **said**" — wow!

Words are extremely powerful, so much so that in Proverbs we learn "the tongue has the power of life and death." Do you realize God doesn't attribute this power to *any* other member of your body or any action you can take? We need to take what we say a lot more seriously!

Quick, careless words slaughter more spirits and lay open more wounds (that are slow to heal) than guns, knives or automobile accidents combined. There is more suffering from unloving words (that may or may not be intended as weapons) than any other kind of suffering in the world. But because these wounds don't bleed, we often use words that cripple and maim others without much thought of the wound we may be leaving.

However, we are too civilized to ignore a bleeding wound. A physical wound that bleeds usually heals with time and a certain amount of care. A wounded heart may take many 'lovings' before any healing takes place and complete healing may never occur on this earth. *Are we bringing forth life with our tongue?*

St. James knew the power of words when he compared the tongue to a powerful (yet relatively small) rudder that steers a huge ship. James went on to say, "with the tongue we praise our God, and with it we curse men, who have been made in God's likeness. Out of the same mouth come praising and cursing. My people, this should not be." We have the choice between positive or negative words and God wants us to consistently use positive ones.

Jesus taught his disciples that, "out of the overflow of the heart the mouth speaks." Every word we say has its origin in our heart — in our thoughts. As you take greater control over your

"Let everyone be quick to hear, slow to speak and slow to anger."
— St. James

thoughts, you will automatically get a better grip on the words that proceed out of your mouth.

When her daughters were very small girls, Mrs. Dwight Morrow gave a high tea at which one of the guests was to be the senior J. P. Morgan. The girls were to be brought in, introduced and ushered out. Mrs. Morrow's great fear was the possibility that Anne, the most outspoken of them, might comment audibly upon Mr. Morgan's celebrated and conspicuous nose. She therefore took pains beforehand to explain to Anne that personal observations were impolite and cautioned her especially against making any comment upon Mr. Morgan's nose, no matter what she might think of it.

When the moment came and the children were brought in, Mrs. Morrow held her breath as she saw Anne's gaze fix upon the banker's most prominent facial feature and remain there. Nonetheless, the introduction was made without incident. The little girls curtsied politely and were sent on their way. With a sigh of relief, Mrs. Morrow turned back to her duties as hostess and inquired of her guest, "And now, Mr. Morgan, will you have cream or lemon in your nose."

What we focus our thoughts on has a tendency to slip out of our mouth!

Our Words are to be:

1. **Gracious**: our words should be always full of grace, "seasoned with salt."
   "Words from a wise man's mouth are gracious, but a fool is consumed by his own lips." — Ecclesiastes
   A hot-headed woman once told John Wesley, "My talent is to speak my mind."

Replied Mr. Wesley, "Woman, God wouldn't care a bit if you buried that talent."

2. **Restrained**: "A man of knowledge uses words with restraint, and a man of understanding is even-tempered." — Proverbs

"He who guards his lips guards his soul, but he who speaks rashly will come to ruin." — Proverbs

We are to be quick to hear, slow to speak and slow to anger.

This reminds me of a cute Dennis the Menace cartoon. Picture this: The family is sitting down to the dinner meal and Dennis is staring intently at a middle-aged female guest. All of a sudden He blurts out, "Mom, I don't see no blue streak when she talks!"

3. **Challenging**: "The words of the wise are like goads, their collected sayings like firmly embedded nails — given by one Shepherd." — Ecclesiastes

A goad is a pointed rod used to urge on an animal — something that spurs.

4. **Appropriate**: "A word aptly spoken is like apples of gold in settings of silver." — Proverbs

"A man finds joy in giving an apt reply — and how good is a timely word!" — Proverbs.

Speaking of appropriate words, I recently ran across this amusing anecdote:

It was a blistering hot day, the house was full of guests, and things weren't going too well. Finally, the hostess got everyone seated for dinner and asked her seven-year-old daughter to say grace.

"But mother," said the little girl, "I don't know what to say."

"Remember not only to say the right thing in the right place, but far more difficult still, to leave unsaid the wrong thing at the tempting moment."
— Benjamin Franklin

"Yes you do," said her mother, "just say the last prayer you heard me use."

Obediently, the child bowed her head and recited hesitantly: "Oh, Lord, why did I invite these people on such a hot day?"

5. **Gentle/Patient**: "Through patience a ruler can be persuaded, and a gentle tongue can break a bone." — Proverbs

6. **Comforting**: "Your words have supported those who stumbled; you have strengthened faltering knees." — Job

   "The Sovereign Lord has given me an instructed tongue, to know the word that sustains the weary." — Isaiah

7. **Edifying**: "Do not let any unwholesome talk come out of our mouths, but only what is helpful for building others up according to *their* needs, that it may benefit those who listen." — St. Paul

   Most of us learned a little rhyme on the playground, "sticks and stones may break my bones but names (words) will never hurt me."

   No matter how confident this is said, it is not true! Names and words can and often do hurt us. They can also put us over the top in life when used in an edifying way!

Results of Speaking the Right Words:

1. **Refreshing and healing**: "Pleasant words are a honeycomb, sweet to the soul and healing to the bones." "The tongue that brings healing is a tree of life, but a deceitful tongue crushes the spirit." — Proverbs

2. **Soothes Anger**: "A gentle answer turns away wrath, but a harsh word stirs up anger." — Proverbs

3. Life: "The mouth of the righteous is a fountain of life." — Proverbs

In his book, "The Awesome Power of Your Attitude," Dale Galloway said, "The reality is that you create the atmosphere you live in by the words you speak. When your words are positive, you produce a creative, loving, positive atmosphere. When you speak negative words you create suspicion, mistrust, and a 'can't-do-anything-right' atmosphere."

"I've got to say no to the good so I can say yes to the best."
— Zig Ziglar

A great way to test the power of uplifting speech is to set aside a day where you greet everyone you meet with a positively encouraging word. Whether it's a friend, neighbor, co-worker, family member or even an enemy — make no exception! You will be amazed at the incredible day you will have following through with this plan. The positive environment you create around you all day will give you abundant energy, not to mention that you can't help getting blessed when you bless others.

Here is a neat measuring stick you can use to gauge your speech:

T — *Is it true?*
H — *Is it helpful?*
I — *Is it inspiring?*
N — *Is it necessary?*
K — *Is it kind?*

If what you are about to say does not pass these tests, keep your mouth closed. *Remember, a closed mouth gathers no feet!*

Talk Nice to Yourself

Do you know what one of the master keys that releases your potential is? It's what you say when you talk to yourself. In my seminar I usually ask the participants, "How many of you talk to yourself?" A small percentage of them will raise their hand. I'm sure those who don't sit there and say to themselves, "No, I don't think I do...now if I were Kevin I'd talk to myself!"

The reality is that we *all* talk to ourselves. And while we talk to others at a rate of approximately 200 words per minute, you're talking to yourself at somewhere around 800 words a minute. We talk to ourself all the time and what we say has an incredible impact on how we feel, what we believe and what we'll achieve.

Words Trigger Pictures

A psychiatrist was concerned that his receptionist's reckless words were triggering the wrong pictures in his patient's mind. He said to her, "When you answer the phone, could you please say, 'We're terribly busy right now,' instead of 'It's a madhouse!'"

Words definitely trigger pictures in our mind's eye don't they? To test this theory out, I don't want you to picture the moon right now. Just keep it out of your mind for a moment. Don't allow a picture of the moon or the Apollo space program to come into your thoughts. Next, don't picture a killer whale. Don't even think of allowing the image of a beautiful Orca whale leaping out of the blue Pacific to enter your mind.

Were you successful? Pretty hard to do, right? I challenge you to remember this the next time you ask someone *not* to do something. Think of how often we give directives to people, especially our children, with "don't" in front of it. "Don't spill your milk." "Don't forget to take out the trash." "Don't write so sloppy." What picture does this trigger in their minds? What emotions? The exact opposite of what we want! Instead, let's remember to give them the picture we want to have happen like, "Thank you for being careful with your milk." "Remember to empty the trash." "Please take the time to write neatly."

Our words *do* bring up pictures that come with various emotions attached depending on what you associate with the pictures. Unpleasant words, generate unpleasant images that bring along unpleasant feelings. Of course the reverse is also true. Words that edify produce beautiful pictures that come with wonderful feelings attached to them!

We actually develop an attitude toward something based on the feelings we experience in relation to the word pictures we see in our mind. In chapter 7 we'll take a more in-depth look at the significance of attitude.

A man attributed the secret of his popularity to one particular word. "Years ago," he said, "upon hearing a statement with which I disagreed, I used to say 'Baloney,' and people began to avoid me like the plague. Now I substitute 'Amazing' for 'Baloney' and my phone keeps ringing and my list of friends continues to grow." It *is* amazing how just using different words can bring about entirely different emotions.

A teacher once asked her class what each of them wanted to become when they grew up. One by one they answered, "President," "a fireman," "a teacher," until it came to Billy's turn.

The teacher asked, "Billy, what do you want to be when you grow up?"

"Possible," Billy responded.

"Possible?" Asked the teacher.

"Yes," Billy said, "my mom is always telling me I'm impossible. When I grow up I want to become **possible**!"

Do you realize that *it is possible* to change the inside image people have of themselves with our words? Let's look at this statement by the German philosopher Goethe, he said, "Treat people as they are and they remain that way. Treat them as though they already were what they can be and you help them become what they're capable of becoming." This compelling statement speaks volumes about helping others (including ourself) change into the people they can become. Our strategically spoken words of encouragement, praise and affirmation play a major role in making this happen.

"If thou thinkest twice before thou speakest once, thou wilt speak twice the better for it."
— William Penn

Sherman Rogers is a man who has written a book about logging in the Pacific Northwest. A story is told about a time when as a young man, Sherman worked in a logging camp. On one occasion the boss needed to be away for awhile and put him in charge.

"What exactly does that mean?" Sherman wanted to know. "Can I fire people?"

"Yes," said the foreman, "And I know what you're getting at. You're going to fire Tony the first chance you get. I know he doesn't get along with anybody. He's nasty and he grumbles. But let me tell you something about Tony. He's been with me eight years. He's the first person to arrive on the job and the last to leave. Nobody has ever had an accident around Tony. His hill is always the safest one to work on."

On the first day of his new responsibilities, Sherman arrived at Tony's hill and announced he had been put in charge.

"I suppose that means you're going to fire me," said Tony.

"Actually, I was," said Sherman, "but the boss told me you're the best workman we have. He said you're the first to come and the last to leave, and there's never been an accident around you."

Sherman was startled to see tears begin to flow down Tony's cheeks. "Why didn't he tell me that eight years ago?" He cried.

Twelve years later, Tony was the head of one of the largest logging companies in the area and he never failed to remind Sherman that it all began on the day he was told what the boss had said about him.

We are all surrounded by people who have no sense of their importance or worth. When we treat them like the person they are capable of becoming, before you know it, they will rise to that level.

Words Can Trigger the *Wrong* Emotions

Just as words can trigger positive emotions, they can all too easily produce negative feelings as well. To test this out I would like you to pause for a moment and think of some of the things that you *have* to do, but don't enjoy doing. For instance, taking out the trash, repairing a leak, paying taxes, and ultimately dying.

"As you believe, so do you speak; and as you speak, so do you act; as you act, so goes your future."

Do you really *have* to take the garbage out? No. You can let it spill over onto the kitchen floor and make a slimy mess. Do you have to repair the leak? No. Buy a larger bucket! Do you have to pay taxes? No. You can move to another country or you can have thirty-five children.

"What?" You say, "Thirty-five children! I *want* to pay taxes!"

Do you **have** to do anything in your life? You really have choices don't you? For every action or decision you choose to make there are consequences. The only 'have to' in life is death, and that has some pretty exciting spiritual ramifications for you and me!

How many weeks in a row can you tell yourself in the fall, "I have to put the lawn chairs away for the winter"? "I should put them away this weekend." How many weeks in a row can you say that without putting your lawn chairs away? What happens? They rot right out there in your yard.

Do you have to be at work by 7:30 a.m. tomorrow? No, of course not; they'll replace you!

"I *have to* be in an 8:00 a.m. Monday morning meeting." Tell your boss what you would rather do than be at the meeting. But first, ask yourself how long you have worked there, not counting Monday?

Why do we choose to use these disempowering words? It's more than semantics. There is literally a push back in your subconscious when you use them. Words play a such a strong role in motivation. You want to choose your words carefully.

Disempowering	**Empowering**
Eliminate:	*Replace With:*
• Have to	• Want to or get to
• Can't	• Choose to learn how
• Must (not)	• Intend to
• Ought (not)	• Decided to
• Should (not)	• Going to

Who is really in control of you? You are! Remember, the vocabulary you regularly use triggers pictures and feelings. It is so releasing to get your life into a 'choose to/want to' state.

Personal Application:

1. Words are either constructive or destructive. Take a few moments to identify some phrases which you are no longer going to use. Remember words are tools that can predict and perpetuate your performance.

   For example:

   "It's going to be one of those days."
   "I can never do anything right."
   "I always catch colds."
   "How can I be so stupid?"

   _____

   _____

   _____

   _____

   _____

   _____

   _____

2. Now let's turn it around. Take each of your negative statements and write out the positive opposite you are going to use from now on.

   For example:

   "It's going to be a great day."
   "It's like me to get things done right."
   "I am healthy and resist colds."
   "God gave me all the brains I need."

   _____

   _____

_____

_____

_____

_____

_____

3. For the next twenty-four hours in particular, pay close attention to your self-talk — monitor what you say to yourself. Try to catch yourself (and others) in the act of 'saying' things right.

"Speak all kind words and you will hear kind echoes."

"What's the biggest room in the world? The room for improvement!"

6 Know Whose You Are
— *Discovering the Image You Are Molded In*

"So God created man in his own image,
in the image of God he created him;
male and female he created them."
— Genesis

So few of us realize the incredible significance of being created in the image of God. When you truly grasp the fact that you are the Creator of the universe's child it will change your life! In this chapter we will look into how a proper understanding of your self-image or self-concept greatly enhances your confidence, your esteem, and ultimately your performance.

A story is told about a farmer who caught a young eagle and brought it home to live among his chickens, ducks and turkeys. He gave it chicken food to eat even though it was an eagle, the king of birds.

Five years later, a naturalist came to see him and after passing through the farm yard, said: "That bird is an eagle, not a chicken."

"You're right," said the owner, "but I have trained and conditioned it to be a chicken. It is no longer an eagle, it is a chicken, even though it measures 15 feet across from one wing tip to the other."

"No," said the naturalist, "it is still an eagle; it has the heart of an eagle, and I will make it soar high up into the heavens."

"I don't think so," said the farmer, "it is a chicken and it will never fly."

They agreed to a test. The naturalist picked up the eagle, held it up and said with great

"We should strive to be the best we can be and to reach the highest levels we can reach.
To do less is to be unfaithful stewards of the life entrusted to us."
— Charles Blake

intensity, "Eagle, you are an eagle; you belong to the sky and not to this earth; stretch forth your wings and fly." The eagle turned this way and that, and then looked down, saw the chickens eating their food, and down he jumped.

The farmer said: "I told you it was a chicken."

"No, it *is* an eagle," insisted the naturalist, "give it another chance tomorrow."

So the next day he took it to the top of the house and said: "Eagle, you are an eagle; stretch forth your wings and fly." But again the eagle, seeing the chickens feeding, jumped down and joined them.

Then the farmer gloated, "I told you it's a chicken."

"No way," asserted the naturalist, "it is an eagle, and I know it has the heart of an eagle; only give it one final chance, and I will get it to fly tomorrow."

The next morning he rose early and took the eagle far outside the village and away from the farm house, to the foot of a very high mountain. The sun was just rising, crowning the summit with gold and causing it to glisten in the joy of the beautiful morning. He picked up the eagle and said to it, "Eagle, you are an eagle; you belong to the sky and not to the earth; stretch forth your wings and fly." The eagle looked around and trembled as if new life were coming into it. Yet it still did not fly. The naturalist then made it look straight at the sun. Suddenly it stretched out its wings, let out a screech and took off, mounting higher and higher into the clear blue sky, never to return to its life as a chicken.

In a similar fashion, we have been created in the image of God, but have been conditioned to

"It's not the qualities you have. It's the qualities you recognize and use that will make the difference"
— Zig Ziglar

think and live at a much lower level. We are to be like the eagle. Don't be content with the life of a chicken — stretch forth your wings and fly!

What Does God Think About Us?

Do we realize **whose** image we are made in? In the book of Genesis we learn that God created mankind, male and female, **in his image**, and **according to his likeness.** We are the only earthly being that can claim this! We are a spiritual being, a free moral agent whose intelligence, perception and self-determination are unmatched on this planet.

The more we understand God and get a revelation of who he truly is, the more we'll become like him. Remember, God wants to live in and through our lives, and all meaningful and lasting change starts on the inside and then works its way out!

The Psalmist said "For you created my inmost being; you knit me together in my mother's womb. I praise you because I am fearfully and wonderfully made; your works are wonderful, I know that full well." In all seriousness, can you say this about yourself? Do you really believe you are *wonderfully* **made**? This is how your Heavenly Father looks at you!

"When you stop and think about what you are worth to God — it can literally take your breath away."
— Kevin Baerg

St. John reminds us "How great is the love the Father has lavished on us, that we should be called children of God! And that is what we are!" In the eighth Psalm, David is musing on the greatness of God and his majestic creation. In light of this he wonders what significance man has in comparison. God's answer is found in verse five. "You have made him a little lower than the heavenly beings (angels) and crowned him with glory and honor." Note that the verse says "a little lower than the angels" **not evolved**

"Capacity and ability constitute accountability and responsibility. We should never be pleased to dwell on a level of existence lower than that on which God has made it possible for us to dwell."
— Charles Blake.

a little higher than the apes! Notice also that God has crowned us with glory and honor. This speaks of the splendor that belongs to God, to his creation, to his kingdom, and now also rests on mankind who is made in his image. This glory and honor is bestowed on us in spite of mankind's smallness in relation to the vast universe. Truly, this view of mankind is higher and more worth-affirming than any other viewpoint in the world.

Speaking of creation versus evolution for a moment, I just came across a great word picture: "For the universe to arise from a point of infinite density to create life purely by accident is about as likely as a tornado accidentally creating a 747 as it whirls through a junkyard." — 'Anthropic Principle' Scientists

I wholeheartedly concur!

Who Do You See in the Mirror?

As I stated earlier, I believe one of the key things that holds us back from using more of our God-given potential is the way we look at ourselves. We all have an image of who we think we are and who we think we are not. Instead of being totally based on the bedrock truth of scripture, it is based on the sum total of all our life's experience. Is this image accurate? Or have we and/or others etched a picture that is anything but a reflection of how God sees us?

Violet Asquith describes a conversation with a young Winston Churchill at the dinner table: "For a long time he remained sunk in abstraction. Then he appeared to become suddenly aware of my existence. He turned toward me with a lowering gaze and asked me how old I was. I replied that I was nineteen. 'And I,' he said almost despairingly, 'am thirty-two already.'

On reflection he added thoughtfully, 'Younger than anyone else who counts, though.' Then savagely, 'Curse ruthless time! Curse our mortality. How cruelly short is the allotted span for all we must cram into it!' He burst into a diatribe about the brevity of life and ended: 'We are all worms. But I do believe that I am a glowworm.'"

I will only agree with Sir Winston that *at our worst* we are most certainly comparable to worms. But I love how his true self-image comes through with the belief that his life was to shine brighter than those around him. He was already confident at a young age that his life was significant, and that a great purpose lay before him.

Many of us can relate to Charlie Brown. One day, Charlie was busy with a woodworking project when Lucy came by and asked: "How's the birdhouse coming along, Charlie Brown?"

He replied, "Well, I'm a lousy carpenter. I can't nail straight. I can't saw straight and I always split the wood. I'm nervous, I lack confidence, I'm stupid, I have poor taste and absolutely no sense of design. So, all things considered, it's coming along okay."

Again, it is impossible to perform consistently in a manner inconsistent with the way you see yourself. You will almost always act in accordance with your current self-image. Your performance will be based on the perception you have of who you are. **You must learn to see yourself *where you want to be* instead of just where you are!** Nothing is more difficult than trying to change on the outside without first changing your thoughts and feelings on the inside. We need to remember the unconditional love of God and his complete acceptance of us as individuals. God thinks much more highly of us than we ever do of ourselves.

I love the story of the little girl who was asked by her Sunday school teacher, "Who made you?"

The little girl replied, "Well, God made part of me."

"What do you mean, God made part of you?" asked the teacher with surprise. "Well, God made me real little, and I just growed up the rest myself."

"I'm so optimistic I'd go after Moby Dick in a row boat and take the tartar sauce with me."
— Tony Campolo

Much of our attitude and self-image is formed as we are raised and may not be what God originally intended for us. A lot of our growing up is done by ourselves and reflects all our experiences both positive and negative.

In the fourth grade (grade four to my Canadian readers), I had a positive experience in the area of athletics. Everyone in our school was tested in six areas of physical fitness and compared to national standards in Canada. There were three levels to aim for; gold, silver and bronze. Before I knew it, I had achieved the gold level in all six events! This qualified me for the Award of Excellence — a 'cool' patch to sew on my jacket and a special certificate signed by the Prime Minister of Canada.

I had suddenly become an excellent athlete, most importantly in my own mind, but also in the minds of those around me. This 'picture' remains with me to this day and affects my daily decisions regarding personal health and fitness. I may not be in the same physical condition as my youth, but I consistently work at keeping in great shape. I went on to win the same award a total of four times over the years, but still look back with a smile on that first victory.

Definition of a Healthy Self-Image

In his book, "Building Your Self-Image," Josh McDowell states, "a healthy self-image is 'seeing yourself as God sees you — no more and no less.' In other words, a healthy self-image means having a realistic view of ourselves from God's perspective, as we are portrayed in the scriptures. I add the phrase 'no more and no less' because some people have an inflated view of themselves (pride), while others have a self-deprecating view of themselves (false humility). Sometimes this is a result of pride and other times a result of a lack of knowledge."

As my grandfather always said, "Keep your chin up...but not out."
— Mick O'Brien

Jesus taught his disciples to love their neighbor as themselves. And that is the problem with the world — so many people do! They have a poor image of who they are, they don't respect and take care of themselves and consequently they treat others in the same fashion. It is only when we have a healthy concept of who we are that we are able to love our neighbor properly.

The Foundation of Your Attitudes

Your self-image is really the foundation of your attitudes.

The Foundation of Significance

We know that in all things God works for the good of those who love him, who have been called according to his purpose. Your feeling of significance will grow stronger and stronger when you truly realize God has a specific purpose for your time on this planet.

The Foundation of Security

St. Paul encourages us by saying, "If God is for us, who can be against us? Can anything separate us from the love of God?" Your sense of security will greatly expand when you dwell on these points:

1. God Almighty is *for you*, not against you.
2. He graciously gives you *everything* you need.
3. *Nothing* can separate you from God's love!

Wow! That does something in my heart! These truths give us tremendous security. We can afford to take risks in life because we are secure in God. Those who are insecure are afraid to risk failure. Those who are secure are honest with themselves and can admit failure. They can ask for help and give it another try. *They have the freedom to change.*

Forgetting the Past

God wants us to forget our past failures and to look for him to do new things in our lives. The book of Isaiah tells us: "Do not call to mind the former things, or ponder things of the past. Behold, I will do something new, now it will spring forth; will you not be aware of it? I will even make a roadway in the wilderness, rivers in the desert." These verses meant so much to Patty and I that we had a beautiful melody of it sung at our wedding.

"The greatest single cause of a poor self-image is the absence of unconditional love."

A man stopped by and visited a family one summer and the father of the family introduced the children to him.

"This is Pete, he's the clumsy one. That's Kathy coming in with mud on her shoes. She's the sloppy one. As always, Mike's last. He'll be late for his own funeral, I promise you."

The dad did a thorough job of gluing his children to their faults and mistakes. People do it to us and to those we love all the time. They remind us of our failures, our errors, our sins

and they won't let us live them down. There are
some people who desperately try to free themselves from their past. They would love a
chance to begin again, but their past seems to
be glued permanently to their lives. When we
don't let people forget their past, when we don't
forgive, we glue them to their mistakes. We
refuse to see them as more than something they
have done. However, when we forgive, we
gently pry the 'doer' of the hurtful deed away
from the deed itself.

When we accept God's forgiveness, "he
separates us from our sins, as far as the East is
from the West." That offense will be wiped
away — 'whited out!' We don't have to stay
glued to our mistakes. The healing power of
God is ours for the asking.

The Danger of Wrong Comparisons

Another great story from scripture that
illustrates these principles is the story of Gideon.
In the book of Judges, the angel of the Lord
introduces Gideon to us by calling him a
"mighty warrior." I honestly believe that Gideon
looked behind him to see just who this angel
was talking to. I bet he was thinking, "It certainly couldn't be me!" Gideon responds with
excuses as he questions God's care of Israel in
light of the current situation. God's reply to
Gideon is basically, 'Go do something about it
and *use the strength I have given you!*'

Then we really get a peek at Gideon's
self-image. "But Lord," Gideon asked, "how can
I save Israel? My clan is the weakest in
Manasseh, and I am the least in my family."

The Lord answered, "I will be with you, and
you will strike down the Midianites as if they
were but one man."

*"However much we
guard ourselves
against it, we tend
to shape ourselves
in the image others
have of us. It is not
so much the
example of theirs
we imitate, as the
reflection of
ourselves in their
eyes and the echo
of ourselves in
their words."*
— Eric Hoffer

You see, Gideon didn't believe he had the 'right stuff.' He compared himself to others in both his immediate family and his extended family and felt he didn't measure up. He didn't think he had what it takes to succeed. But God knew what he was doing and he saw the potential warrior in Gideon. *What does God see in you that is hidden? What precious gems are tucked away inside of you?*

Compared to Whom?

Who are we supposed to compare ourselves to? What is to be our standard?

George Sweeting tells this story, "In an Italian city stands a statue of a Grecian maiden with a beautiful face, a graceful figure, and a noble expression. One day a poor little peasant girl came face to face with the statue. She stood and stared, and then went home to wash her face and comb her hair. The next day she came again to stand before the statue, and then to return home once more. This time she mended her tattered clothing. Day by day she changed, her form grew more graceful, and her face more refined, till she greatly reflected the famous statue she had been gazing at. She was transformed in appearance!" Just so, the spiritual minded person must each day seek to conform to the perfect image of our Heavenly Father.

The best comparison we can make is to look intently at God and his character and continually work at chipping away the parts of our life that don't match his likeness. When we compare ourselves with the others around us we tend to get ourselves in trouble. If all I do is try to be better than the next person, what good is that if my performance is still below the potential God has for me?

"Success is not measured by how you do compared to how somebody else does. Success is measured by how you do compared to what you could have done with what God gave you."
— Zig Ziglar

You've probably heard it said, "the easier it is to be good, the harder it is to be great." Why? Because when things come easy we rarely work harder or stretch farther than necessary. *Don't let your 'good' become the enemy of your 'best.'*

We need to test our own actions, and have a healthy sense of pride in who God has made us to be — without comparing to someone else. Don't compare with others, compare with your own best self. Who is your own best self? *It is the image of God!*

It bothers me when religious people say there is no such thing as healthy pride. Furthermore, they tell us that we are to have no self-esteem, and a low self-image. Perhaps it comes from a misunderstanding of what scripture really says, or what the words themselves mean. All I know is that what I have learned about God's heart for people tells me otherwise.

> *"People with humility don't think less of themselves — they just think about themselves less."*
> — Ken Blanchard

Personal Application:

Five Steps to a Healthy Self-Image:

1. Get your thought life under control. As you learned in the last chapter, you've got to talk nice to yourself — only words that build you up and give you grace. Your self-talk is where a lot of your image comes from. Remember, as you think in your heart (deep down) that's who you are!

2. Allow God to cleanse and heal you from all past sins, mistakes, failures and the wounds others have inflicted on you. When you really stop to think about it, we all have lived with a measure of 'dysfunction' at some point in our lives. After all, 'Normal' is only a setting on your washing machine — right?! Put the past behind

you. Choose to begin your life anew with a clean slate. Remember, every moment is a fresh new start with God! The Spirit of God wants to work inside of you and be a constant helper in all of these steps.

3. Spend as much time as you can in fellowship with God. Talk to him, listen to him and spend time being quiet before him. Read the scriptures — they are his words of instruction in how to live and they reveal how he 'sees' you. Remember, the more you see God, spend time with him and get a revelation of who he really is, the more you will become like him.

"No one can make you feel inferior without your consent."
— Eleanor Roosevelt

4. Only receive from others what you want to dwell upon. You are responsible for the 'entries' you record in your memory banks. If someone says negative things to you, take any grains of truth and let the rest roll off your back. Let the garbage go in one ear and out the other!

5. Learn to do at least one thing *well* so you can get some wins under your belt and experience a measure of success. This will increase your confidence and empower you to excel in other areas of your life.

This last point is perfectly illustrated by a story I have heard about Dr. James Dobson. Apparently, when James was a teenager in high school, he went through that awkward phase that so many go through. You know, when you feel like you've got more feet than hands! Anyway, he really wasn't excelling in any area of his life — especially athletically. Then someone taught him how to play tennis and he learned it well enough to make the tennis team at school. The team worked hard together and as a result won a championship for their school. This whole experience gave Dobson such a boost of confidence that he parlayed that success into other areas of his life. He learned to do something well and now look at what God has done in and through his life and the work of Focus on the Family around the world!

*"What lies behind
you and what lies
before you pales
insignificant when
compared to what
lies within you."*
— Ralph Waldo Emerson

7 The Wind Beneath Your Wings
— Gaining Altitude with a Rising Attitude

"Our attitude is the primary force that will
determine whether we succeed or fail"
— *John Maxwell*

Next to having a vital relationship
with God, nothing is more
essential than having a positively
great mental attitude. Your attitude can make or
break you, bring healing or sickness, happiness
or misery, peace or distress, success or failure.
The great thing is, the choice is up to you! In this
chapter you will learn how changing your
attitude can change your life forever. No one
forces your attitude upon you! You alone decide
how you will respond to any and every situation
in life. You have the power, privilege and
responsibility from God to choose what is right
— to choose life over death. It all starts with
your attitude.

*"Ability is what
you're capable of
doing. Motivation
determines what
you do. Attitude
determines how
well you do it."*
— Lou Holtz

John Maxwell says, "Most people are very
close to becoming the person who God wants
them to be." I heartily agree with him, in fact,
you're probably only an attitude or two away as
you'll soon discover!

Attitudes also have a big impact on how we
feel. It was 9 a.m. on a gloomy Monday
morning and the elevator was overflowing.
As the car started up, the elevator man began
humming a tune and dancing a little jig. One
passenger seemed particularly irritated by the
man's mood and snapped, "What are you so
happy about today?"

The man replied happily, "Well, Sir, I ain't

never lived this day before."

For many people, you'd think they would have to win the lottery before they could be happy! Sometimes we set the 'bar' for happiness so high it is almost impossible to achieve it.

Are You a Thermometer or a Thermostat?

Thermometers and thermostats have related, but quite different functions. Both have to do with how hot or cold a place is, but the similarity ends right about there. A thermometer merely reflects its surroundings; **it does nothing to influence them.** Thermometers do one thing very well. They report conditions of the moment. What they don't do well is affect the future. Thermostats on the other hand, seek to influence their surroundings and make them comply to the set temperature by turning on the furnace or the air conditioner according to the need. Are you a thermometer or a thermostat? Do you accept the status quo as being the norm or do you seek to make a difference by working to change your environment?

"The greatest discovery of my generation is that people can alter their lives by altering their attitudes of mind."
— William James

Your self-image (what you believe about yourself) and your attitudes make up the internal thermostat that governs the achievement of your life. It keeps your behavior within a comfortable range of performance known as your 'comfort zone.' If you perform under *or higher* than this range, you will experience tension, anxiety and internal conflict. This is your creative subconscious trying to help you stay in alignment with the image you hold of yourself. It wants to get you back 'where you belong' in the rut of your comfort zone. *Remember, a rut is just a grave with the ends kicked out!*

Thermostats have a built in comfort zone as

well that usually ranges around two degrees above and below the set temperature. As long as the temperature stays within that range, nothing happens. If it goes below, the heater will come on. If it goes above, the air conditioning comes on. You don't want the air to come on in your life and cool you off! You want to learn how to raise the set temperature and stay in hot pursuit of the purpose God has for you.

In chapter four, we studied the thought process. In chapter five, we explored the power of the tongue and how your self-talk impacts who you think you are and the attitudes you possess. In the last chapter, we looked more closely at your self-image and how it is formed through your experiences and the way you think and talk to yourself about those experiences.

"A person cannot travel within and stand still without."
— James Allen

In this chapter, you will learn how to properly use your attitudinal thermostat to raise your internal temperature for greater achievement in life.

One of the key benefits of reading and applying the principles in this book is that it gives you the tools to change the internal picture or image you have. When your image changes, your behavior will automatically change to match your new image. Again, this is your creative subconscious at work, helping you to act like *your perception* of who you are.

When you change your image first, rather than focusing on the behavior, your attitudes, actions and habits will fall in line with your image. Therefore you truly are changing from the inside out, and best of all, *you don't even have to try that hard.* First you change your self-image, and then you start acting like the new you! That is what this chapter is really all about.

What is an Attitude?

An attitude is a pattern or a habit of thinking. It is the direction in which you lean. Attitudes are inward feelings expressed in our outward behavior. It's how you see things: Is the glass half-full or half-empty? Is there an 80% chance for sunshine or a 20% chance of rain?

An American was out touring in the Sahara dressed only in a bathing suit. A Bedouin gazed at him in amazement.

"I'm going swimming," the tourist explained.

"But the ocean is eight hundred miles away," the Bedouin informed him.

"Eight hundred miles!" The American exclaimed with a huge smile. "Boy, what a beach!"

It's all in how you look at things. Some people find difficulty in every opportunity, while others find opportunity in every difficulty. Which group do you tend to side with?

Some folks today have the attitude that the whole world stinks. One time a grouchy old grandpa decided to enjoy a little nap. His grandson thought he would create a little fun with this situation so he placed some especially stinky limburger cheese in his grandpa's mustache.

"Hardening of the attitudes is the most deadly disease on the face of this earth."
— Zig Ziglar

Grandpa awoke with a snort, stumbled out of the bedroom and declared, "This room stinks!" He quickly tore through the house shouting louder, "This whole house stinks!" He ran out on the porch and yelled at the top of his lungs, "The whole world stinks!" The truth be known, it was grandpa who stunk! The problem could be found right under his own nose. Most of the time when we begin to think everything stinks around us, the root cause of the problem is not external — in the world or with others, but internal — *with ourselves.*

John Maxwell adds this to the definition of attitude:

> *"It is the 'advance man' of our true selves.*
> *Its roots are inward but its fruit is outward.*
> *It is our best friend or our worst enemy.*
> *It is more honest and more consistent than*
>   *our words.*
> *It is an outward look based on past*
>   *experiences.*
> *It is a thing which draws people to us or repels*
>   *them.*
> *It is never content until it is expressed.*
> *It is the librarian of our past.*
> *It is the speaker of our present.*
> *It is the prophet of our future."*

"Always hold your head up, but be careful to keep your nose at a friendly level."
— Max L. Forman

Still another way to look at attitude is to check into some flying terminology. When an aircraft is in flight its attitude refers to the position of the plane in relationship to the horizon. A 'nose-down' attitude occurs when an aircraft is diving. When an airplane is climbing, the nose of the plane, and therefore its attitude, is pointed up. The attitude of the airplane directly affects its performance and the direction it is going. The attitude of the plane is so important that pilots keep a close watch on the special attitude indicator on the instrument panel.

"The great thing in the world is not so much where we stand as in what direction we are moving"
— Oliver Wendell Holmes

What we expect from life can be summed up in the attitude of our life's 'airplane' so to speak. If the nose of our airplane is pointed up, we will climb higher; if it is pointed down, we better change our attitude lest we end up in a crash and burn scenario.

How does this apply to you? Do you have an attitude indicator — a gauge for measuring your attitude? Does your attitude really affect your performance and direction? What can you do if you're in a 'nose-down' attitude and losing altitude fast? *How do you change your attitude?*

The Secret

We don't have control over all of life's circumstances, but we can control the attitudes we manifest in response to challenging situations. One of the keys is to learn to be content whatever the circumstances — whether you are in need or have plenty. When my wife Patty and I were just engaged and on a missions trip to England with a puppet team, we learned what it was to be in need. We were so broke that when one of our teammates offered us a lick on their ice cream cone, we got excited! When another offered us one of their french fries, we rejoiced! In comparison, we're now enjoying the 'plenty' aspect of life as well, having had the privilege of designing and building our dream home.

"If you can't see the bright side, polish the dull side."

I believe the secret of being able to choose our attitude no matter what the situation lies not in our own strength, but relies on the power of God in our lives. We have the ability to adjust our attitude. It doesn't come automatically — it is a *learned* behavior.

Other than God, no one has ever had a perfect attitude. All of us need an attitude adjustment from time to time. Getting back to the aircraft model, we learn that all airplanes have to trim their attitude. The word *trim* represents the balance of the aircraft in flight. All airplanes need continual fine-tuning or trimming of their attitude in order to obtain optimum performance and reach the desired destination.

When the weather of life gets rough, what really matters is what happens *inside* you, not what happens *to* you. Remember, the testing of your faith develops perseverance. Perseverance adds maturity and completeness to our lives — it brings us to a place where we are not lacking anything. I like the idea of not lacking anything! I hope that picture can encourage you to have a better attitude toward the trials that come your way.

The oft-quoted Victor Frankl, a survivor of the holocaust, said this. "The last of the human freedoms is to choose one's attitude in *any* given set of circumstances." He had more authority to speak about this than most of us ever will have! We do get to *choose* our attitudes.

"People are just about as happy as they make up their minds to be."
— Abraham Lincoln

Nothing that anyone has done to us (or not done for that matter) excuses us of a bad attitude. We aren't responsible for anyone else's attitudes or actions but God definitely holds us accountable for our own. We need to get beyond the 'being hurt' or the 'dysfunctional' stage and get on with God's plans for our lives without regret or excuse. We're not controlled by some worldly force. God has given us the ability to overcome our circumstances through the power of his Spirit. As I stated earlier, let's deal with the past once and for all and move on with our lives. More healing will come as we go about fulfilling the destiny we were created for.

The Importance of Attitude

How important is your attitude? Take a few moments and think of the most successful people you know or are aware of. (Feel free to use your own definition of success rather than someone else's when you think of the people).

What are the qualities that have helped them be successful? Are they enthusiastic, energetic, dedicated, hard-working, honest, compassionate, or persistent? Do you realize that these qualities are all attitudes or directly linked to an attitude? In fact when I ask the same question of people from all walks of life at my seminars, and they list qualities of successful people, over 90% of them are straight attitudes. No wonder attitude is so important in life, regardless of what you plan to do.

Chuck Swindoll has composed a masterful 'creed to live by' with his piece on attitude:

"We can't cause the wind to blow in the direction we want, but we can adjust the set of our sails to take us where we want to go."

Attitude

"The longer I live, the more I realize the impact of attitude on life. Attitude, to me, is more important than facts.

It is more important than the past, than education, than money, than circumstances, than failures, than successes, than what other people think or say or do. It is more important than appearance, giftedness, or skill. It will make or break a company...a church...a home.

The remarkable thing is we have a choice every day regarding the attitude we will embrace for that day. We cannot change our past...we cannot change the fact that people will act in a certain way. We cannot change the inevitable. The only thing we can do is play on the one string we have, and that is our attitude...

I am convinced that life is 10% what happens to me and 90% how I react to it. And so it is with you...we are in charge of our Attitudes."

Attitude Check

Have you had an attitude check recently? How would you rate your current overall attitude?

☐ Never been better
☐ Going higher
☐ Ho-Hum
☐ Heading down
☐ Never been worse

The Change Process

— *How to create a new self-image by changing attitudes and habits.*

1. **Examine your present attitudes and habits** and determine the ones you really want to change. Make a list leaving space to write by each one.

2. **What is the positive opposite** of the attitude and/or habit? (e.g. Impatient – patient, disorganized – organized, procrastinate – take action).

3. For each attitude or habit you wish to change, think about **how you developed the attitude** in the first place — all habits start as an attitude. What events happened in your life? What things were said to you? How did they make you feel? Write this down on your list.

4. Knowing that an attitude is a habit pattern of thinking; **what thoughts do you want to change** that are linked to the negative attitude you want to replace? What patterns of self-talk do you want to re-script? Jot these down as well.

5. Now that you know what you want to change, **get leverage on yourself** by

"A happy person is not a person in a certain set of circumstances, but rather a person with a certain set of attitudes."
— Hugh Downs

answering two questions:

a. **What will happen if you don't change** this attitude and the resulting habits and behavior? What pain will you experience this year, in five years and over a ten year period if you don't change?

b. **What great things will happen as a result of making the change?** What joy and pleasure will it bring into your life this year, in five years and over the next ten years?

6. **Get a 'faith picture' of yourself already accomplishing the change** and lock on to it. In order to make change easy, you want to see yourself already achieving the desired result in faith, before it happens in reality. Write this out in the form of a 'faith reminder.' *(Faith reminders are more thoroughly explained in the next chapter).*

Personal Application:

On the following page you will find a Change Process Worksheet. Please complete the first five steps of the change process with at least one attitude or habit that you wish to change. In the next chapter, we'll look into the sixth step more in depth and learn how to properly design a faith reminder for this part of the change process.

For an example of a completed Change Process Worksheet, please see page 190. (For additional blank forms, visit www.inspiration4u.com).

"Attitudes are contagious: Is yours worth catching?"

"Life can be likened to a grindstone. Whether it grinds you down or polishes you depends on what you are made of."

Change Process Worksheet

1. List the attitude and/or habit you really want to change.

2. What is the positive opposite of this attitude and/or habit? *(e.g. impatient – patient, disorganized – organized).*

3. How did you develop this attitude in the first place? What events happened in your life? What things were said to you?

4. Knowing that an attitude is a habit pattern of thinking; what thoughts do you want to change that are linked to the negative attitude you want to replace?

5. Get leverage on yourself:
   a. What will happen if you don't change this attitude and the resulting behavior? What pain will you experience:

   This year:

   In five years:

   In ten years:

   b. What great things will happen as a result of making the change? What joy and pleasure will it bring into your life:

   This year:

   In five years:

   In ten years:

6. Write out a 'faith reminder' with you already having accomplished the change and lock on to it.

Sow a thought
Reap an attitude
Sow an attitude
Reap an action
Sow an action
Reap a habit
Sow a habit
Reap a character
Sow a character
Reap a destiny!

8 Evidence of Things Unseen
— Using the Dynamic Duo of Faith and Imagination

"Now faith is the substance of things hoped for, the evidence of things not seen."

— *Hebrews*

Without faith it is impossible to please God. It is also virtually impossible to accomplish anything of significance without extending faith and using the amazing imagination God gave you. In this chapter you will learn how to create 'faith reminders.' Partnering with God, they will empower you to change attitudes and habits in order to positively impact your life.

Writer Oscar Schisgall shares the following story that tells how stepping out in faith radically changed the course of his life:

"When I was a young writer with a very uncertain income, I went into a quiet park to contemplate a serious problem. For four years I had been engaged but didn't dare to marry. There was no way of foreseeing how little I might earn in the next year; moreover, we had long cherished a plan of living and writing in Paris, Rome, Vienna, London — everywhere. But how could we go 3000 miles away from everything that was familiar and secure, without the certainty of some money now and then?

At that moment I looked up and saw a squirrel jump from one high tree to another. He appeared to be aiming for a limb so far out of reach that the leap looked like suicide. He missed — but landed, safe and unconcerned, on a branch several feet lower. Then he climbed to

"All I have seen teaches me to trust the Creator for all I have not seen."
— Ralph Waldo Emerson

his goal, and all was well.

An old man sitting on the bench said, 'Funny, I've seen hundreds of 'em jump like that, especially when there are dogs around and they can't come down to the ground. A lot of 'em miss, but I've never seen any hurt in trying.' Then he chuckled, 'I guess they've got to risk it if they don't want to spend their lives in one tree.'

I thought, 'A squirrel takes a chance — have I less nerve than a squirrel?'

We were married in two weeks, scraped up enough money for our passage and sailed across the Atlantic — jumping off into space, not sure what branch we'd land on. I began to write twice as fast and twice as hard as ever before. And to our amazement we promptly soared into the realm of respectable incomes. Since then, whenever I have to choose between risking a new venture or hanging back, I remember those squirrels and sometimes I hear the old man on the park bench saying, 'They've got to risk it if they don't want to spend their lives in one tree.'"

The Foundation for Change

Faith is the foundation for change in our lives. From deciding to believe in God, to changing the tiniest thought, attitude, or habit — your faith plays a key role. As you would expect, the scriptures have plenty to say when it comes to this topic.

The book of Hebrews states, "Now faith is being **sure** of what we hope for and **certain** of what we do not see." Faith is not positive wishing while holding back the seeds of doubt — *it is surety and certainty!*

We can't even please God without faith. It is

"Part-time faith, like a part-time job, cannot fully support you."

"Faith without a measure of risk isn't faith at all."

the starting point for getting anywhere in our relationship with him.

Recently I heard an appealing analogy for the faith experience. A small boy was flying a kite high up in the sky. Soon a low-drifting cloud encircled the kite and hid it from view.

"Some things have to be believed to be seen."

A man passed by and asked the little boy, "What are you doing with that string in your hand?"

"Flying my kite," the child responded.

The man looked up at the sky and saw only the cloud in an otherwise clear sky. "I don't see a kite up there. How can you be sure that there is a kite on the end of that string?"

The child replied, "I don't see it either, but I know my kite is up there because every once in a while I feel a little tug."

Has God tugged on your string lately?

Remember, "we live by faith, not by sight" and "hope that is seen is no hope at all. Who hopes for what he already has?"

We are accustomed to reading the scriptures on faith and relating them to our relationship with God. I would like for you to look at them from an additional perspective. Are you comfortable using these same principles to help you change your behavior? Most people have never thought of this before. They know they are to believe God for provision and protection, but they don't really exercise their faith when it comes to becoming the person they are capable of being.

"Positive thinking is the hope that you can move mountains. Positive believing is the same hope but with a reason for believing you can do it."
— Zig Ziglar

Making a one time decision to change an attitude or achieve a goal is not enough. In order to change easily and permanently, a clear picture in your mind needs to be developed of the desired end result you are after. This takes faith — seeing the unseen! In order to enjoy the type of life you want, you need to think, talk and conduct your life, in alignment with the faith picture of who you are yearning to be. This requires keeping this picture consistently in front of you.

"It's not what God can do, it's what we will believe him for!"

You Become What You Believe

We do become what we believe. Several years ago a man named Leon Festinger did some research. He came up with a theory called 'cognitive dissonance.' Basically, he says that humans are more rationalizing than they are rational. In other words, we gather data to support or rationalize our dominant beliefs, whatever they may be, in order to prove we're not absurd.

If you see yourself as an angry person, you gather data to support this belief and consequently, you'll find yourself falling into the trap of losing your cool too often.

You might say, "I'm just a very angry person; I know I am, my dad was angry and so was my grandfather. I've always been angry. Even when I ask God to help me with my anger, I find myself getting angry at him!"

Now that's what I call a dominant belief! You will actually gather data in your subconscious mind to support and perpetuate that belief *even though you may not want it in the first place.*

Let's look behind the scenes into your subconscious mind as we continue with the anger example. Since your dominant belief is that you are an angry person, let's represent it with a large capital '**A.**' It looms ominously compared to the willpower behind your goal to change and become calm, which we'll represent with a tiny 'c'. Now, when you have just a little bit of willpower versus this great big subconscious belief, who do you think wins? There's no contest, your subconscious belief will win most of the time. If that's true, what if we knew how to take that little old '_c_' and swell it? What if we knew how to make it big — really big? What if we knew how to develop a new belief system?

Is there any likelihood that being angry or being calm is a chromosome? I think not! In reality it's an attitude, a choice that gained momentum and became a habit. Again, don't get hung up on the fact that you've had it for 27 years. Think of it like you've had it one year 27 times. _You formed the attitude over time, then it formed you._

How Do You Use Your Faith to Change?

You use **faith** to change your attitudes and self-image. You develop what Bob Moawad, Chairman of Edge Learning Institute calls, "an internal ad campaign," with structured words that create _belief without evidence._ Remember, if you don't see yourself achieving your goals or changing bad habits in your mind first, you will never see it happen in real life.

"Sorrow looks back, worry looks around, faith looks up."

Why does this work? As I mentioned earlier, as you have experiences in life, you form 'three dimensional' attitudes about who you are through words triggering pictures that are colored with emotion or feelings. Researchers have discovered that when you are relaxed, any thought or picture focused on in your mind, with vivid imagination and emotion, is stored as reality in your brain. In other words, your subconscious mind cannot tell the difference between something you have experienced and something you have vividly imagined. The limbic system colors every experience you have with feelings and emotion, whether they really happened or you intensely imagined them.

This imagined experience will have anywhere from ten to sixty times more impact than having the actual experience. In other words, one relaxed minute of vivid imagery along with the appropriate emotions, stores up cells of recognition in the neuron structure of the brain that can equal from ten to sixty minutes of actual life experience. Wow!

You can test this out if you like. Either read the following paragraph to someone or have them read it to you while you follow the instructions.

"Imagination is more important than knowledge."
— Albert Einstein

Lemon Taste Test

Close your eyes for a moment and imagine that you are about to cut open a lemon that is in your hand. The pungent aroma of the lemon fills your nostrils as you bring down the knife and cut right through the middle of the lemon. It's a juicy one! As you pick up one of the halves, the juice runs over your fingers. Without any physical movement, in your imagination only, bring the lemon up to your mouth. Feel your arm coming up. The lemon is right in front of you now. Run your tongue across the face of the half lemon. Oh my, does it have pucker power or what! Now sink your upper teeth into the soft fleshy part of the lemon and squeeze in the cool, sour juice.

Open your eyes. Did your mouth (or someone else's) begin to water? Mine just did while I wrote this down. But there is no lemon! That is a physiological response to your vivid imagination. If we had an electromyogram (muscle-sensing graph) attached to your arm, we could have actually measured movement in your muscles. You can literally program your muscles for later activities.

Visual Motor Behavior Rehearsal (VMBR)

As a result of the research along these lines that Masters and Houston started close to 50 years ago, people all over the world have increased their effectiveness by using these principles. You may have heard of this by another name — Visual Motor Behavior Rehearsal (VMBR). It is one of the key techniques that athletes in the '90's are using to improve their 'game.' From skiers, to bowlers, to hockey players and football stars, most of the top-notch competitors are using VMBR to give them the slight edge. For example, Jack Nicklaus rehearses every shot in his mind before he physically hits the ball.

My favorite athlete in the world is Wayne Gretzky. I am passionate about the game of hockey, and Wayne is my hockey hero. He holds more NHL records than any player in history. Wayne had some interesting things to say about visualizing things in his autobiography, "Gretzky."

"We taped a lot of famous pictures to our locker room door: Bobby Orr, Potvin, Beliveau, all holding the (Stanley) Cup. We'd stand and look at it and envision ourselves doing it. *I really believe if you visualize yourself doing something, you can make that image come true.*" In another passage he said, "Probably my fondest memory is picking up the Stanley Cup the first time. As a kid, I watched all the great players pick up that Cup. *I must have rehearsed how I would do it ten thousand times.*" I'm glad you did Gretz!

One of my special dreams is to have lunch with Wayne and two of my special friends who are also huge fans of the 'Great One.'

"Our imagination is the only limit to what we can hope to have in the future."
— Charles F. Kettering

The Slight Edge

In the 1989 PGA tour of 23 tournaments, the difference between first place and ninth place in terms of the money earned was fairly substantial. Tom Kite, the first place finisher earned $1,395,000 while Chip Beck in ninth place won just $694,000. That's a difference of $701,000, and I don't know about you, but it takes me a long time to earn that much!

The surprise comes when you look at their average scores. One would expect the scores to have a similar disparity in comparison with the earnings. Not so. Tom Kite averaged 70.42 strokes per round for first, while Chip Beck averaged 70.60 per round for ninth. That is a difference of just 18 hundredths of a stroke. That's less than a 'gimme!' Talk about the slight edge making a huge difference.

Little things can make a big difference. Just a few little adjustments often can change your life.

Conquer Fear with Faith

Another way of looking at faith is dwelling *where you want to go*, focusing on *what you want to have happen* in your life. Fear is dwelling on what you don't want to have happen. I like this little acronym for the word fear:

False
Evidence
Appearing
Real

"Faith hears the inaudible, sees the invisible, believes the incredible, and receives the impossible."

The African impala can jump to a height of over 10 feet and cover a distance of greater than 30 feet. Yet these magnificent creatures can be kept in an enclosure at any zoo with only a three foot high wall. Apparently, the animals will not jump if they cannot see where their feet will fall. That is where faith comes in! Faith is the ability to trust when we cannot see. With faith, we are freed from the flimsy enclosures of life that try to entrap us in our fear.

The Power of Your Imagination

In an interview in 1974, NBA Hall of Famer, Pete Maravich said, "I don't want to play 10 years in the NBA and die of a heart attack at age 40." In 1984, having played exactly 10 years in the NBA, Pistol Pete died of a heart attack while playing a half-court pickup game in Pasadena. Whoa — the power of predictions! What are you focusing on today — this moment?

"We learn from experience that not everything which is incredible is untrue."
— Cardinal de Retz

Here's another amazing but true story to show how powerful your imagination is. A railway employee in Russia accidentally locked himself inside a refrigerated boxcar, which can be a hazardous to your health! Since he was unable to attract the attention of anyone outside, he resigned himself to his fate, which he thought would be freezing to death.

As he felt his body becoming numb, he recorded the story of his approaching death in sentences scribbled on the wall of the boxcar.

"I'm becoming colder...still colder now. Nothing to do but wait..."

How's this next prediction?

"I am slowly freezing to death...Half asleep now. I can hardly write..."

Finally, he says, "These may be my last words."

And they were for when the car was opened, they found him dead. But the temperature of the car was only 56 degrees! Does that seem warm for freezing? The freezing apparatus had been out of order. There was no physical reason for his death. There was plenty of air — he hadn't suffocated. He was the victim of his own illusion. His conclusions were all wrong — he was so sure he knew! The power the mind has over the body can produce effects which seem almost unbelievable.

Now remember, what are we experts at? Reporting where we are: "I can't do anything with this 11 year-old of mine."

"People at work are driving me crazy."

"We're coming up on the holidays, and I have to get gifts for everyone and rush through all the activities."

We observe and report to our subconscious, unaware of what we're doing to predict and perpetuate what *we might not want to have happen*.

You've probably have heard it said, people who want to get well have a better chance than people who don't. It has been proven that large numbers of people in rest homes actually put off dying until after January 1st. They look forward to Thanksgiving, Christmas and New Years Day. Why, you ask? They might get extra love and attention, more visits, gifts, and so on. For most people it truly is a happy time of year — a time to look forward to!

Use Imagination to Your Advantage

Do you think you have ever been influenced by advertising in your buying decisions? Of course you have! We're being influenced every day. It's a multi-billion dollar industry. I wonder if you can finish any of these:

"Plop plop, _____ _____, oh, what a relief it is."

"How do you spell relief? _ _ _ _ _ _ _."

"You deserve a _____ _____ at

McDonald's, we do it all for you."

"You've got the right one baby ___ - _____"
I guess you laid awake all night and
memorized those, didn't you? No, the spaced
repetition of millions of dollars in TV and radio
advertising did it automatically. Corporations
spend more than one million dollars per 30
second ad on Superbowl Sunday. Does it work?
You bet it does! I don't really care to see
another Bud Bowl in my lifetime, but I've heard
that after those ads go on the air, sales of
Budweiser go up about twenty-five percent!

Using Words as Tools

Since advertising works so well, we're going
to design some of our own internal ads that
we'll call faith reminders. All of us have used
little reminders to help us out in life. These
reminders will combine your faith and
imagination to produce the right picture in your
mind, thus triggering the desired emotional
impact.

We're going to use words as the tools in
these ads. They're neither true nor false, positive
or negative, constructive or destructive, except
by how you use them. Can you use words to
build? Can they be used to destroy? Consider
them as any other tool, a screwdriver for instance. When you go to the store, do you ask
for true or false screwdrivers? No. You say, "I
need a large Phillips, a square head or a torx."

The word 'affirmation' is a term you may
have heard of before. Affirmations are simply
statements of fact or belief about reality as you
perceive it. You have been making affirmations
all of your life. It's just another word for self-
talk. Affirmations such as, "You know, I'm just a

*"The people who get
on in this world
are the people who
get up and look for
the circumstances
they want, and, if
they can't find
them, make them."*
— George Bernard Shaw

little tired of reading." Or, "When is he going to get to the main point?" Or on the other hand, "I'm really enjoying this book." "It's having a big impact on me." "A lot of people I know sure could benefit from this information." These are all affirmations. Remember, we're always talking to ourselves.

"A head hung in despair cannot scan the horizon for God's provision."

Instead of letting random affirmations shape your attitudes and habits, why not get creative and structure your own word tools to help build your dreams? We're going to call them by a specific name that is well suited to this book: 'Faith Reminders.' As you'll see, they really are statements of faith designed to create the picture and accompanying emotion of the end result you wish to achieve. In order for them to work, it takes faith and the creative imagination God gave you.

Once again, look at your words as neither true nor false, but as tools. They will predict or perpetuate your performance based on the fact that they trigger images and emotions, which directly affect your attitudes and habits.

"Well, Kevin, you might say, these faith reminders just don't seem natural. They just don't seem to flow naturally."

"God is looking for those through whom he can do the impossible — what a pity that we plan only the things that we can do by ourselves."
— A.W. Tozer

What was natural at birth? Eating, sleeping, responding to stimuli and filling diapers. After that, let's face it, it's all learned. Was learning to walk natural or easy and were you good at it right away? Was speaking a language natural? Were you good at it? How about feeding your-self — natural? Were you good at it? Were you excellent in your first attempts at any other skill you've picked up in your lifetime?

Faith + Imagination = Reality

God has given us an incredible imagination and he wants us to use it. Noah did, Abraham did, Solomon did. All the heroes of the faith used their faith in God and creative imagination to accomplish great things in his name.

When Goliath reared up his ugly head and taunted the army of Israel, all the soldiers were thinking, "He's so big we can never kill him." David looked at the same giant through his eyes of faith and thought, "He's so big I can't miss!" David envisioned killing Goliath from the first moment he saw him defy the armies of God.

"Anything worth doing is worth doing poorly until you learn to do it well."
— Zig Ziglar

Anybody that accomplishes anything in the world uses faith pictures. Whether they are believers in God or not, the principle still works, although I dare say being a believer definitely gives us a considerable advantage.

Do you think Annie Sullivan didn't see herself getting through to Hellen Keller long before it happened? Do you think the Wright brothers didn't fly in their imagination long before their first flight at Kittyhawk? We know that Edison pictured a glowing light bulb in his mind literally thousands of times before it finally became a reality.

Remember, there are always two creations — first in the mind, with a vision or a faith picture, and secondly with the physical fulfillment of the vision.

What Can Faith Reminders Do for Me?

"Practice within, when you're without."

1. They help feed your mind with the picture of where you **can** be.

2. They help your subconscious believe that this new picture of where you can be is where you **already are**.

3. They raise your self-image and create positive expectations.

4. They cause a positive conflict for your creative subconscious to resolve, urging you to act like the new picture of you.

Again, you're using your faith — belief without evidence — to create a new image in your mind through the use of structured words. These words will trigger positive pictures and feelings at the subconscious level resulting in a new self-image. Your subconscious now expects you to act like the new you, creating the dissonance necessary to bring about the positive conflict for your creative subconscious to resolve.

"You move toward and become like the thoughts you hold uppermost in your mind."
— Bob Moawad

How to Design Your Faith Reminders

How you structure the words in your faith reminders is very important since you are attempting to change the dominant belief in your subconscious mind. You want the statements to have a lot of impact!

1. **Make it personal** — you are the central figure in the reminder.
   Effective: *"I enjoy spending time in prayer daily."*
   Non-Effective: *"Spending time in prayer is a good thing to do."*

2. **Make it positive** — describe what you desire, rather than what you don't want.
   Effective: *"It feels terrific being totally organized at home and at work."*
   Non-Effective: *"I am no longer disorganized."*

3. **Make it present tense** — state it as though you already have it — extend your faith!

Effective: *"I enjoy consistently catching my family, friends and colleagues in the act of doing things right."*
Non-Effective: *"I am going to get better at catching my family, friends and colleagues in the act of doing things right."*

4. **Attach positive emotion** — be creative with vivid pictures.
Effective: *"I have abundant joy serving faithfully in my community."*
Non-Effective: *"I am serving faithfully in my community."*

5. **Be Realistic** — use words like 'consistently' and 'regularly' instead of the inflexible 'always' and 'every time.'
Effective: *"I regularly spend one wonderful night each month on a special date with my spouse."*
Non-Effective: *"I always spend one night every week on a special date with my spouse."*

6. **Be Specific** — specify what you want by using words as targets.
Effective: *"It feels great averaging a goal and an assist per hockey game this season."*
Non-Effective: *"It feels great scoring more goals and assists during this hockey season.*

7. **Include a scripture verse** — where applicable.
Effective: *"I feel awesome consistently getting up early to pray and seek the Lord on a daily basis."*
"Give ear to my words, O Lord, consider my sighing. Listen to my cry for help, my King and my God, for to you do I pray. Morning by morning, O Lord, you hear my voice; morning by morning I lay my requests before you and wait in expectation" (Psalm 5:1-3).

"It is only by risking our persons from one hour to another that we live at all. And often enough our faith beforehand in an uncertified result is the only thing that makes the result come true.
— William James

Personal Application

"The days ahead are filled with changes which are my challenges. I will respond to these opportunities with the confidence that my life will be better because of them. With God all things are possible."
— John Maxwell

At the end of the last chapter, on the Change Process Worksheet, I asked you to complete the first five steps of the change process outlined there with at least one attitude or habit that you wanted to change. Now I would like you to go pack to page 101 and complete the sixth step of the change process by designing an appropriate faith reminder. Remember to use the above guidelines as you create it.

Once you are finished, I recommend transferring your faith reminder to a 3 x 5 card or to your daily planner in order to facilitate reviewing it several times each day.

For an example of a completed Change Process Worksheet, please see page 190.

9 Create a Compelling Future
— Harnessing the Power of Goal-Setting

"What would you do if you knew you could not fail?"

— Dr. Robert Schuller

Are you using the power of goals to create a compelling future for your life? Few indeed are the people who have taken the time to write down their God-given dreams. Setting goals is an integral part of charting your future course in life. In this special 'hands on' chapter, you will have the opportunity to step aside from any past limitations and let your lifetime goals literally pour out of you.

I want to start off by asking you a simple yet powerful question that I often pose to people. What would you do if nothing stood in the way from reaching your goals? In other words, what would you do if you **had** the time, money, health, energy, knowledge and skills required to accomplish your dreams?

"Most of us are so busy doing what we think we have to do, that we do not think about what we really want to do."

— Robert Percival

God Has Plans For You

The prophet Jeremiah states "'For I know the plans I have for you,' declares the Lord, 'plans to prosper you and not to harm you, plans to give you hope and a future.'" This is one of my favorite verses in the scriptures because it so clearly portrays the loving heart of our Heavenly Father. It falls completely in line with my belief that God is *for* each and every one of us. He longs to give us hope and bless us with a wonderful future.

On the front porch of his little country store in Illinois stood Abraham Lincoln and his partner. Business had all but disappeared, and Berry asked, "How much longer do you think we can keep going?"

Lincoln answered, "It looks like our business has about winked out." Then he continued, "You know I wouldn't mind so much if I could just do what I want to do. I want to study law. I wouldn't mind so much if we could sell everything we've got and pay all our bills and have just enough left over to buy one book, Blackstone's commentary on English law, but it doesn't look possible."

"The ladder of life leads only upward for those with the courage to attribute their every success to the power of the Spirit."

Just then, a strange looking wagon came up the road. The driver drove it up close to the store porch, and the man looked up at Abraham Lincoln and said, "I am trying to move my family West and I'm out of money. I've got a good barrel on here that I could sell for fifty cents." Abraham Lincoln's eyes went along over the wagon and came to the wife looking up at him pleadingly, with her face thin and emaciated.

Abraham Lincoln ran his hand into his pocket and took out, according to him, "the last fifty cents I had," and said, "I reckon I could use a good barrel."

All day long the barrel sat on the porch of that store. Berry kept chiding him about it. Late in the evening, Abraham Lincoln walked out and looked down into the barrel, and saw some things in the bottom of it — papers that he hadn't noticed. His long arm went into it, fumbled around, and hit something solid. He pulled out a book and stood petrified. It was the 'Commentary on English Law' by Blackstone.

Now these are Abraham Lincoln's words: "I stood there holding the book, looking up toward the heavens. There came a deep impression on me that God had something for me to do. He was showing me now that I had to get ready for it. Why this miracle otherwise?"

Delight Yourself in the Lord and...

"Delight yourself in the Lord and He will give you the desires of your heart." More people have 'stood' on this verse from the Psalms than perhaps any other. Most of us like to focus on just the second half of that promise and believe God will give us our desires. However, we must not forget there is a condition. We are to delight in him first. That means putting the Lord first in your life. Of course, as you do this, your desires are much more likely to conform to his desires anyway. Before you know it, the verse comes true — as God blesses you with your heart's desire!

In 1977, a single mother named Glenna Salsbury, with three young daughters, needed to have her dreams rekindled. She went to a seminar where she learned the 'I x V = R' principle: Imagination multiplied by vividness equals reality in your subconscious. Sound familiar? The seminar speaker shared how the mind thinks in pictures, not in words. He encouraged the participants to vividly picture their desires in their mind, and watch them become reality.

Aim at Heaven and you will get the earth thrown in. Aim at earth and you will get neither."

This concept rang true with Glenna and she remembered God's promise in the Psalms — He wants to give you the desires of your heart. She decided to take her written prayer list and turn it into a picture book. She cut up old magazines and placed the pictures that represented the desires of her heart in an expensive photo album. Then she waited expectantly to see how God would answer her dreams.

She was very specific with her pictures which included:

1. A good-looking man.
2. A woman in a wedding gown and a man in a tuxedo.
3. Bouquets of flowers (She's a romantic).
4. Beautiful diamond jewelry (She said "I rationalized that God loved David and Solomon and they were two of the richest men who ever lived!").
5. An island in the Caribbean.
6. A lovely home.
7. New furniture.
8. A woman who had recently become vice-president of a large corporation. (At the time Glenna was working for a company that didn't have any women officers. She wanted to be the first).

Eight weeks later she was driving down the freeway when a beautiful red and white Cadillac came up in a lane beside her. She looked at the car, the driver smiled at her, she smiled back and then realized she was in deep trouble.

He followed her for fifteen miles and she said, "It scared me to death! I drove a few miles, he drove a few miles. I parked, he parked... and eventually I married him!"

"Progress always involves risks. You can't steal second and keep your foot on first."

Well to make a long, but beautiful story short, Jim started sending her roses, in fact for two years every Monday morning she received a long-stemmed red rose and a love note from him. She also found out his hobby was collecting diamonds — big ones — and he wanted to decorate somebody. Glenna says, "I volunteered!" Their wedding was at Laguna Beach, California and included the gown and tuxedo. At Jim's suggestion, they honeymooned on St. John's Island in the Caribbean. A year

later they moved into their gorgeous new home
furnished with the elegant furniture she had
pictured. By the way, eight months after she
created her dream book, she become the
Vice-President of Human Resources!

Glenna shares, "In some ways this sounds
like a fairy tale, but it is absolutely true. Jim and
I have made many picture books since we have
been married. God has filled our lives with the
demonstration of these powerful principles of
faith at work."

She challenges people to, "decide what it is
that you want in every area of your life. Imagine
it vividly. Then act on your desires by actually
constructing your own personal goal book.
Convert your ideas into concrete realities
through this simple exercise. There are no
impossible dreams. And, remember, God has
promised to give his children the desires of their
heart."

*"Hold fast to
dreams, for if
dreams die, life is a
broken winged bird
that cannot fly."*
— Langston Hughes

God Wants You to be Specific!

Years ago, before I was married, one of my
leaders in Youth With A Mission (YWAM)
challenged me to make out a very specific
prayer list of all the things I needed and desired.
I immediately wrote out a list of things that
ranged from finances for a plane ticket, to some
deodorant and toothpaste I desperately needed
and didn't have money for!
I also wrote down that I wanted a 35mm camera
with a 55mm lens. I hesitated to put down the
55mm lens specification, but that was the size
my dad used and I wanted to be specific.
Shortly after compiling this list, I began a casual
friendship with one of the other students in the
school. I soon learned that she had been fairly
involved in photography, but wasn't doing

*"Don't just think it
— ink it!"*

much with her camera at the time. I told her of my interest in taking some nice pictures and she loaned her camera to me. Lo and behold, when she showed it to me, it was a 35mm camera with a 55mm lens!

I thought to myself, "Lord, this is great, she's going to give it to me, isn't she?"

"It's not what you get, it's what you become."

Well I enjoyed using her camera, but she appeared to be in no hurry to give it to me. Week after week went by and she still hadn't given it to me. Finally, after six weeks, I decided to take matters into my own hands and I asked her to marry me. That way, I got the camera and the girl — what a deal!

The moral of the story for all you single women out there: *Don't give anything to a man until he asks you to marry him!*

It's so fun to look back over lists of goals that I have written and see how God has brought so many to pass in my life. He is a faithful Father who dearly loves to bless his kids! If you don't have this picture of God in your life yet, today is the day to start receiving it.

What's Holding You Back?

In our world there are 14 peaks above 26,000 feet (8000 meters). If we dropped you off at the top of any of these peaks you'd die in minutes from a lack of oxygen. Only one man has climbed all 14 peaks, he is Reinhold Messner from Northern Italy. He's arguably the greatest climber in the world. He has ascended many of these peaks without the aid of oxygen, including Mount Everest! In fact, he climbs either by himself or with a small party, avoiding the usual expedition entourage of hundreds of porters, numerous climbers and guides plus thousands of pounds of supplies.

"Whether you think you can or think you can't, you're right"
— Henry Ford

In October, 1986 he conquered the 14th peak, called Makalu, at 27,756 feet on the third attempt. He said, "It's not easy when you walk 25 steps, stop and breathe deeply ten or twenty times, then take a few more steps."

Experts wondered how could he perform such physical exertion with so little oxygen. Doctors have examined him only to find that he is not some kind of bionic man, although he does have the physique of an above-average marathoner. Many others have the capacity to do what he does. So why don't they do it?

> *"A winner is someone who sets their goals, commits to achieve those goals, and then pursues their goals with all their ability."*

Another alpine climber says what makes Reinhold Messner different is what he calls 'creative innovation.' He went on to say that in most human endeavors there is a wall which most people call 'impossible,' and they come to it and stop. Then someone comes along like Reinhold with a wonderful imagination and determination and he or she laughs at the wall and moves beyond it. In the process they become more than they ever dreamed possible.

Are you afraid to succeed, afraid to make your dreams a reality? Have you hit the wall called 'impossible'? Perhaps you are now doubting whether your dream is really from God. Good dreams come from God! Why would the devil give you a good dream?

> *"Remember that you are unique. If that is not fulfilled, then something wonderful has been lost."*
> — Martha Graham

When God calls you to do something, you can't just look at yourself and what you can or can't do. **You've got to look at what God has placed uniquely in you**, follow him and he will empower you for the task!

Denis Waitley says, "Goals we can reach with little or no effort have no pulling power. They're not the stuff from which winners are made. The excitement of reaching toward a challenging goal is often greater than the actual achievement. The joy is more in the reaching than in the grasping. Your goals must be demanding, requiring knowledge, effort, and performance to accomplish. With an honest assessment of your talents and skills, you can set goals that are realistic, believable and worth working for."

Jesus taught his disciples, "whatever you ask for in prayer, believe that you have received it, and it will be yours." What could be more empowering than that? Use your faith in God and the strength he has given you to blast through any obstacle you face!

"Attempt something so impossible that unless God is in it, it is doomed to failure."
— John Haggai

Remember to Live Today!

The only danger in goal-setting is getting so caught up in your goals that you fail to enjoy the place where you are right now. So many times you see people who believe they will finally be happy when they achieve this goal or accomplish that plan. However, when they reach the goal or fulfill their plan, they often find little fulfillment from it. They don't realize that, "The journey *is* the reward." as Steve Jobs, co-founder of Apple Computer liked to express.

"When I get married, then I'll be happy!" "When we have children, then I'll be fulfilled!" "When I get that new job, then I'll be satisfied!" "When we build our new home, then I'll really be thrilled!" People who talk like that don't understand that, "It's the hunt, not the kill, that's the thrill," as my friend, Bob Moawad says.

"The foolish man seeks happiness in the distance, the wise grows it under his feet."
— James Oppenhiem

Remember that all you really have to live for is today — the moment before you now. Yesterday is gone forever and tomorrow is promised to no one. Yes, you've got to plan for the future and dream big dreams for tomorrow, but make sure that you **live today!**

Why is Setting Goals so Important?

1. Goals activate your built-in data filtering system.

Think back to the fourth chapter where we looked at your built-in data filtering system. Without goals, your mind doesn't know what data is valuable to you. Life is like a huge database of information that's impossible to assimilate unless you enter the 'search criteria' on the computer screen. Your goals become the selection criteria for your mind. This kicks your filtering system into high gear parsing the billions of bits of information that bombard you daily, turning up only items that are valuable for the attainment of your goals.

2. Goals give us targets to shoot for.

Who wants to play a game of hockey, soccer or basketball without any goals? Just try putting up a blank basketball backboard without the net and see how long your kids take shots at it. Goals prevent boredom and the resulting delinquency in our lives that comes with 'directionless' living.

You may have heard that the Olympian, Wilma Rudolph passed away in 1994. She was born in a shack in the backwoods of Tennessee to a porter and a cleaning lady. She was a premature baby born at four and one half pounds. She had an extremely large family — she was the 20th of 22 children! At age four she contracted polio and scarlet fever, that left her with a partly paralyzed left leg. Doctors told her parents she would never walk again without a brace. But Wilma had a mother who constantly

"When I'm on the ice, I can barely see the goalie. It's an attitude. If you ask a fifty-goal scorer what the goalie looks like, he'll say the goalie's just a blur. A five-goal scorer can tell you the brand name of the pad of every goalie in the league. I'm seeing the net, he's seeing the pad."
— Wayne Gretzky

told her that she could do whatever she wanted to do with her life. All she needed to do was have faith, persistence, courage and a never-give-up spirit. So at the age of nine, Wilma did away with the brace.

"Every great accomplishment was once an impossibility."

Four years later, she finally developed a rhythmic stride that enabled her to run. At 13, she entered her first race and came in dead last. She wouldn't give up. Finally she began to win consistently. At 16, Rudolf won a bronze medal in the 400-meter relay at the 1956 Olympics in Melbourne, Australia. Another four years later, when she was the mother of a 2 year-old, she made it to the 1960 Olympics and won three gold medals, despite running all three events with a sprained ankle. She was the first woman to win 3 gold medals in track and field at the same Olympics!

What Does God Think About Goals?

Goals have been around since the beginning of creation. Remember, God is the ultimate big dreamer! He mapped out the entire universe beforehand, including mankind and our abilities.

"All things are possible for those who believe God for them. Not easy, but just within reach!"

Proverbs tells us to plan our way but know that God will direct our steps. God knows that nothing is accomplished without a goal or a plan and the corresponding actions to bring it to fulfillment. The big question is not whether God has goals, but rather, *what are God's goals and his plans for my life!*

Principles for Effective Goal-Setting

1. Balance your goals.
2. Prioritize your goals.
3. State your goals in a positive fashion.
   (What you want to have happen, not what you are trying to avoid.)

4. Clearly define your goals on paper and make them specific.
5. Focus on the exciting end result you desire. Remember, you don't need to know how to get there.
6. Set realistic time limits, but don't get 'term-paper syndrome' and wait till the last minute to try and meet your deadline.
7. Keep your goals to yourself or at the most, share them only with someone who can help you attain them or who will strongly encourage your endeavor.
8. Review and update your goals regularly. Keep them in front of you and make sure you're still on track. Remember, success is a journey, not a destination.

"The people who know their God will be strong and carry out great exploits."
— Book of Daniel.

In order to emphasize this last point, I like to share the following story:

It was a fog-shrouded morning, July 4, 1952, when a young woman named Florence Chadwick waded into the water off Catalina Island. She intended to swim the channel from the island to the California coast. Long-distance swimming was not new to her. She had been the first woman to swim the English Channel in both directions. The water was numbingly cold that day. The fog was so thick she could hardly see the boats in her party. Several times sharks had to be driven away with rifle fire. She swam more than 15 hours before she asked to be taken out of the water. Her trainer tried to encourage her to swim on since they were so close to land, but when Florence looked, all she saw was fog. So she quit — only one-half mile from her goal.

"Success is moving toward personal, worthwhile, predetermined goals which are in alignment with your vision, mission and values."

Later she said, "I'm not excusing myself, but if I could have seen the land I might have made it." Many times we also fail because we lose sight of the goal.

Two months after her failure, Florence Chadwick walked off the same beach, into the same channel and swam the distance, setting a new speed record. This time she clearly saw the land — she kept her eyes on the goal. Maybe that's why St. Paul said, "I press on toward the goal to win the prize for which God has called me heavenward."

Keep your goals before you! Writing them down and filing them away until next year won't do much to help you attain them.

Who Says it's Impossible?

Years ago, new engineer recruits to General Electric's lamp division were welcomed with an unusual initiation assignment. They were asked to figure out a way to frost the inside of a light bulb. This was a totally bogus assignment meant to be a big joke, because everyone knew it was impossible. Nevertheless, a 'wet-behind-the-ear' newcomer, Marvin Papkin took the task seriously and not only did he discover a way to frost bulbs on the inside, he also developed an etching acid that produced small rounded pits on the surface rather than sharp depressions. This made each bulb stronger. No one told him it was *impossible* so he went ahead and did it!

"Somebody said that it couldn't be done,
But he with a chuckle replied
That maybe it couldn't, but he would
*   be one*
Who wouldn't say no 'till he tried.
So he buckled right in with the trace of
*   a grin*
On his face. If he worried, he hid it.
He started to sing as he tackled the thing
That couldn't be done and he did it.

"We cannot discover new worlds without the courage to lose sight of the shore."

"If you have that flame of a dream down inside you somewhere, thank God for it, and do something about it. And don't let anyone else blow it out."
— Rich DeVos

Somebody scoffed: "Oh, you'll never
do that;
At least no one ever has done it;"
But he took off his coat and took off his hat
And the first thing he knew he'd begun it.
With the lift of his chin and a bit of a grin,
Without any doubting or quiddit,
He started to sing as he tackled the thing
That couldn't be done, and he did it.
There are thousands to tell you it cannot
be done,
There are thousands to prophesy failure;
There are thousands to point out to you,
one by one,
The dangers that wait to assail you.
But just buckle right in with a bit of a grin,
Then take off your coat and go to it;
Just start in to sing as you tackle the thing
That 'cannot be done,' and you'll do it."
— Edgar A. Guest

"Make no little plans; they have no magic to stir men's blood and probably themselves will not be realized."
— Daniel Burnham

Jack Canfield tells a great story about his friend, Monty Roberts. Monty was the son of a travelling horse trainer and as such moved from stable to stable, and ranch to ranch, training horses.

In his senior year of high school, a teacher gave him the assignment of writing a paper about what he wanted to accomplish after graduation.

"It doesn't matter how big the rock is. If you keep pounding, it's going to break."

Monty proceeded to write out a seven page description of a dream horse ranch. He took great pains to include all the specifications including a diagram of 200 acres with all the buildings and track in place. He also produced a detailed floor plan of the 4000 square foot dream house.

He put a lot of effort into this paper and anxiously awaited his grade. The teacher returned it 2 days later with a large red 'F' on the front of it and a note telling Monty to see him after school.

"Why did you give me an 'F'?" Monty asked in frustration.

The teacher replied, "This dream is totally out of reach for a young man like yourself. You come from a travelling family. Where are you going to come up with the money and necessary resources? How will you buy the land, the breeding stock, and pay the stud fees? This is impossible — you could never do it!"

Then to add insult to injury, the teacher added, "I will consider changing your grade only if you rewrite this paper around a goal that is realistic."

Monty went home and thought over what the teacher said for a whole week. He even discussed it with his parents who encouraged him to go with his heart.

Finally, the young man decided to not make any changes and he turned in the very same paper. "You can have your 'F' but I'll stick with my dream," he declared to the teacher.

Well, Monty went on to achieve his dream, which was made even sweeter years later when the same teacher brought 30 kids to camp out at his 'dream' ranch for a week.

As he was leaving the teacher said, "Years ago when I taught you, I was somewhat of a dream stealer. Back then I stole many a youthful dream. I'm glad you had enough guts not to give up on yours."

Has anyone stolen your dreams? Have you somewhere along the way lost the big ideas of your youth? Don't give up, follow God's tug on your heartstrings no matter what. What are some dreams that you would like to resurrect?

"People who say it cannot be done should not interrupt those who are doing it."

"Keep dreaming no matter what anybody says. What matters is what you say to yourself."
— George Foreman
(46 year old heavyweight champion of the world).

'I Wish-I-Woulda'

One rainy Saturday afternoon, a young man 15 years of age named John Goddard decided he had heard one too many adults say how much they wished to have accomplished more with their life. He said to himself, "I'm not going to let this happen to me!"

So he sat down at the kitchen table and wrote out over 127 goals. Since that time, he has accomplished more than 85% of those goals! Let's take a look at some of them: "Explore the Nile, Amazon, and the Congo rivers; climb Mount Everest, Mount Ararat, and the Matterhorn; land on and take off from an aircraft carrier; ride an elephant, camel, ostrich and bronco; write a book; read the Bible from cover to cover; circumnavigate the globe; parachute jump; retrace the travels of Marco Polo and Alexander the Great; run a mile in five minutes..."

If you don't have a dream, how are you going to have a dream come true?

I found the following quote in a magazine article about John's adventures:

"There's a wellspring of determination in each one of us, and if it is tapped, you feel almost invincible. You feel, 'I am going to do this.' Even if everyone tells you it's impossible, you are going to prove that it isn't. It's not an egocentric thing at all. It's just a feeling that you are a human being. You've learned what the human mind and body and spirit can do — and you do it."

— John Goddard

"Goals are nothing more than dreams with deadlines."

Personal Application:

Perhaps some dreams have been flooding your mind as you have been reading. *(Hopefully the right kind of dreams)!*

"Seldom do we exceed our expectations; even if the opportunity arises, we generally fail to take advantage of it."
— Bob Moawad

Most people spend more time planning a two-week vacation than they devote to planning their goals and future course in life. I would like for you to take some action and spend at least 20-30 minutes writing down your goals as a first step toward planning your life. Try to get back into a child like mode and imagine you are writing out your Christmas wish list. In other words, don't be practical!

To help you balance your goals, you will see space by each of the major areas of potential. *I challenge you to list at least five goals in each of these categories.*

Beside each goal, jot down when you'd like to see yourself achieving it, e.g., within 1, 3, 5, 10, or 20 years. Remember, you don't need to know how you're going to pull it off right now — *just dream!* Allow no limitations!

So sit back and dream big dreams for God, and have fun identifying your lifetime goals. May this list become your future journal! Write as rapidly as possible.

"The only way to fail is to not try something!"

My Lifetime Dreams

1. Spiritual/Personal Growth Goals:

_____

_____

_____

_____

_____

_____

_____

_____

_____   *"Attaining the goal is*
                                                 not the greatest
_____   *reason for achieving.*
                                                 What the goal makes
_____   *of you while you're*
                                                 attaining it is."
_____

_____

2. Relational (Family & Friends) Goals:

_____

_____

_____

_____

_____

_____

_____   *"If you have a*
                                                 dream, give it a
_____   *chance to happen."*
                                                 — Rich DeVos
_____

_____

3. Vocational Goals:

"To aim is not enough — you must hit the target. Be very sure your target is worthy of the energy expelled."

_____

_____

_____

_____

_____

_____

_____

_____

4. Financial/Material Goals:

"The past cannot be changed, the future is still in your power."
— Hugh White

_____

_____

_____

_____

_____

_____

_____

_____

_____

5. Recreational Goals:

_____

_____

_____

_____

_____

_____

_____

_____

"I would rather attempt to do something great for God and fail, than to do nothing and succeed."

6. Physical/Health Goals:

_____

_____

_____

_____

_____

_____

_____

_____

_____

"Knowing where you're going is all you need to get there."
— Carl Frederick

"Live your life each day as you would climb a mountain. An occasional glance toward the summit keeps the goal in mind, but many beautiful scenes are to be observed from each new vantage point. Climb slowly, steadily, enjoying each passing moment; and the view from the summit will serve as a fitting climax for the journey."
— Harold V. Melchert

7. Miscellaneous Goals:

_____

_____

_____

_____

_____

_____

_____

_____

_____

10 Lights, Camera...Action!
— *Developing and Implementing Your Action Plan*

"May He give you the desire of your
heart and make all your plans succeed."
— *Psalms*

bsolutely nothing is accomplished
without someone taking action. The
best goals in the world are meaningless
without a plan to achieve them and the decision
to take action. In this chapter you will learn
how to take one of your key goals and catapult
it into a plan of action. This will help you
implement your important goals into daily life.

Charlie Brown is at the plate.

"Strike three!" The umpire barks.

He has struck out again and slumps over to
the bench.

"Rats! I'll never be a big-league player. I just
don't have it! All my life I've dreamed of playing
in the big leagues, but I know I'll never make
it."

Lucy turns to console him. "Charlie Brown,
you're thinking too far ahead. What you need to
do is set yourself more immediate goals."

He looks up. "Immediate goals?"

Lucy says, "Yes. Start with this next inning
when you go out to pitch. See if you can walk
out to the mound without falling down!"

We too, need to have immediate goals —
goals we can work on today, that will help us
reach our dreams for tomorrow. Many of our
dreams are big tasks that can appear too huge
to tackle. How do you eat an elephant? One
elephant burger at a time!

*"If one advances
confidently in the
direction of his
dreams, and
endeavors to live
the life which he
has imagined, he
will meet with a
success unexpected
in common hours."*
— Henry David Thoreau

The Importance of Planning

God is the ultimate planner. The book of Psalms states, "Many, O Lord my God, are the wonders you have done. The things you planned for us no one can recount to you; were I to speak and tell of them, they would be too many to declare." Wow — I get excited when God talks that way about us! Just imagine what God has up his sleeve for you and me — and you know that God has mighty big sleeves!

"Winners can tell you where they are going, what they plan to do along the way and who will be sharing the adventure with them."
— Dennis Waitley

Do you remember the 1984 summer Olympic games in Los Angeles? Did you watch America's Florence Griffith Joyner (Flo-Jo), Carl Lewis, and Jackie Joyner-Kersee win multiple gold medals in track in field? Remember all the worry before the games of crime and terrorism, and yet how peaceful and wonderful they turned out to be?

Think for a moment. Where were you living? Who did you hang around with? What were you like? What were your dreams and aspirations at that time? If someone were to have asked you, "Where will you be in 15 years?" What would your answer have been? How have things turned out — are you today where you wanted to be 15 years ago? Time can sure pass by quickly!

"Many are the plans in a man's heart, but it is the Lord's purpose that prevails."
— Proverbs

There's no use in crying over spilled milk, or for that matter, continuing to glory in the victories of the past. The future is before you now. Today is the only day you have for sure. How are you going to live the next decade of your life? How are you going to live *today* to create the tomorrow you're dreaming of? What actions can you take *today* that will help you fulfill the destiny God has planned for you? Now is the time to plan and strategize for your next 10 years — not once they're over. **Carpé Diem** — *we must seize the day!* The year 2000 is almost upon us, where will you be then? Who will you have become?

Years ago a young boy was growing up in Cleveland, in a home that he later described as "materially poor but spiritually rich." One day a famous athlete, Charlie Paddock, came to his school to speak to the students (he was a character in the movie "Chariots of Fire"). At the time Paddock was considered 'the fastest human being alive.'

He told the children, "Listen! What do you want to be? You name it and then believe that God will help you be it." The boy decided that he too wanted to be the fastest human being on earth. He went to his track coach and told him of his new dream.

His coach told him, "It's great to have a dream, but to attain your dream you must build a ladder to it and take action. Here is the ladder to your dreams. The first rung is **determination**. The second rung is **dedication**. The third rung is **discipline**. And the fourth rung is **attitude**!"

This young boy was none other than Jesse Owens and he went on to win four gold medals in the Berlin Olympics as a result of putting action into his vision. He broke the world record in the 100 and the 200 meter dash. His broad jump record lasted for twenty-four years. Dreams and action — what a powerful combination!

"The wisdom of the prudent is to give thought to their ways."
— Proverbs

The Importance of Action

Life will be no better than the plans you make and the action you take. No one exemplifies this more than God. He is a God of action! He has incredible vision, detailed plans and impeccable execution! He finishes what he starts

"Even if you are on the right track, you'll get run over if you just sit there."

— he acts on his word. We are to be like him in this. For we have learned that faith without action is dead. We are to prepare our minds for action! Our actions are a reflection of what we truly believe.

I recently heard a statistic that less than 20% of the members in most church congregations do 80% of the work. The other 80% must be sitting around, waiting to hear, "Well done, thou good and faithful spectator."

All too often, we act as if we're sitting at a traffic light that's red, and we wait for a green light before we do anything! I believe God would rather have us live as if we have the green light and keep going until he puts on the red light.

Many people are so concerned with attaining God's "perfect" will for their lives that they are afraid to step out and do something new. They fail to realize that God is more than able to let them know when they're heading down the wrong path. If you earnestly desire to follow God's will for your life, (even if it leads you in the opposite direction of where you want to go) don't you believe God will make his plans clear to you? Of course he will!

The prophet Isaiah said, "And your ears will hear a word behind you, 'This is the way, walk in it,' whenever you turn to the right or to the left." In other words, make the decision to act on your goals and dreams first. Then, start making the turn in that direction, listening for that "word" from behind you (or inside you) to confirm your guidance.

Using Failure to Your Advantage

In the 1820s, Gail Borden, Jr. was a journalist in the Texas territory who coined the phrase,

"Chance favors the prepared mind."
— Louis Pasteur

"Deeds, not words shall speak to me."
— John Fletcher

"Many are called but few get up."
— Oliver Herford

'Remember the Alamo.' However, his real ambition was to invent a way to condense food so that it would stay edible for a long time.

Said Borden: "I mean to put a potato into a pillbox, a pumpkin into a tablespoon and a watermelon into a saucer." At every opportunity, he would experiment on guests, serving concentrated soups and foods. For the 1850 California Gold Rush, Borden invented the dehydrated meat biscuit. However, it was a boat trip home from England that sparked 'The Idea,' an idea born out of tragedy.

On board ship, Borden saw children die as a result of drinking contaminated milk. He vowed to dedicate his life to find a way to make milk safe for human consumption. Through his experiments with meat biscuits, Borden knew food could be kept fresh over long periods of time if moisture was reduced. He put a gallon of milk in a kettle and boiled off the water. The experiment failed as the milk had an unpleasant, burnt taste.

While visiting a Shaker colony in New York, Borden found the answer — he saw maple sugar condense in a vacuum-sealed pan. Using the vacuum-sealed pan, less heat was needed to evaporate, reducing the burnt taste. It worked, and the U.S. Army placed the first big order for 500 pounds of condensed milk. Borden did more than invent a process and start what is now a multi-billion dollar company — he founded the modern day dairy business.

These words are inscribed on Borden's tombstone: "I tried and failed. I tried again and succeeded."

When you read about the lives of great people you consistently discover that they have experienced some degree of failure in their

"Everyone who's ever taken a shower has had an idea. It's the person who gets out of the shower, dries off and does something about it who makes a difference."
— Nolan Bushnell

"I have not failed 10,000 times. I have successfully found 10,000 ways that will not work.
— Thomas Edison
(after trying an experiment 10,000 times).

lives. Actually, most of them began their careers as less than best.

The music teacher of the great Polish pianist, Ignace Paderewski told him his hands were too small to master the keyboard.

Henry Ford forgot to put a reverse gear in his first automobile.

"I am not discouraged, because every wrong attempt discarded is another step forward."
— Thomas Edison

The author of the book, 'Little Women,' Louisa May Alcott, was told by her family that she should become a servant or a seamstress.

Louis Pasteur was ranked 15th out of 22 students in chemistry and was labeled a mediocre undergraduate pupil.

Abraham Lincoln is a prime example of someone who kept on trying until he succeeded. Born into poverty, Lincoln faced defeat throughout his life. He lost eight elections, failed twice as a businessman and even suffered a nervous breakdown.

But Lincoln was a champion and he knew the only time you really fail is when you give up and quit. The following is an outline of Abraham Lincoln's 'failures' on his path to the White House:

"The person who never made a mistake never made anything."

- 1831 — Failed in business.
- 1832 — Defeated for Legislature.
- 1833 — Second failure in business.
- 1836 — Suffered nervous breakdown.
- 1838 — Defeated for Speaker.
- 1840 — Defeated for Elector.
- 1843 — Defeated for Congress.
- 1848 — Defeated for Congress.
- 1854 — Defeated for Senate.
- 1856 — Defeated for Vice-President.
- 1858 — Defeated for Senate.
- 1860 — **Elected President**.

"The path was worn and slippery. My foot slipped from under me, knocking the other out of the way," Lincoln said, after losing a Senate race. "But I recovered and said to myself, 'It's a slip and not a fall.'"

Our attitude is the key to whether we allow our failures to make or break us. Persistence in the face of failure is a sign of a winning attitude, because winners never quit!

Did you know that even the scriptures are full of heroes with grass stains on their knees. Abraham lied twice about his relationship with Sarah. Jacob connived his own brother out of his birthright. Early on, Moses murdered a man and then later disqualified himself from entering the promised land. A young Joseph was foolish enough to proudly share his dreams with the wrong people, at the wrong time. David, "the man after God's own heart," committed the unthinkable by taking Uriah's wife and then murdering him as well. An utterly depressed Elijah, prayed that he might die, right after an incredible victory and display of God's power.

"Precious little comes out just right the first time. Failures pothole the road to success."

We all have our areas that don't measure up to God's perfection. Everyone has failed at something at least once. But thanks be to God that he is merciful and forgiving. He loves to give us that second, third or even that 490th chance (70x7)!

Tony Robbins says, **"the past doesn't equal the future."** And you know what, he's right! Just because things haven't worked out the way you planned thus far has no bearing on what happens tomorrow. Everyone who has achieved a measure of success in their lives knows the importance of pursuing their vision and dreams, even if all the pieces to their puzzle aren't yet falling into place.

"It is the combination of reasonable talent and the ability to keep going in the face of defeat that leads to success."
— Zig Ziglar

The Power of Persistence

A young boy was trying to learn to ice skate. He had fallen so many times that his face was cut, and the blood and tears ran together. Someone, out of sympathy, skated over to the boy, picked him up and said, "Son, why don't you quit? You are going to kill yourself!"

"Failure is the line of least persistence."

The boy brushed the tears from his eyes and said, "I didn't buy these skates to learn how to quit; I bought them to learn how to skate."

When you meet with defeat, don't ever quit. Stanley Jones liked to share his motto for life, "When life kicks you, let it kick you forward!"

St. Paul knew all about this. He said: "We are pressed on every side by troubles, but not crushed and broken. We are perplexed because we don't know why things happen as they do but we don't give up and quit. We are hunted down, but God never abandons us. We get knocked down, but we get up again and keep going." What a great motto for living!

"Press on. Nothing in the world can take the place of persistence. Talent will not; nothing in the world is more common than unsuccessful men with talent. Genius will not; unrewarded genius is almost a proverb. Education will not; the world is full of educated derelicts. Persistence and determination alone are omnipotent." This quote by President Calvin Coolidge has become quite popular, although I dare say he must have forgot God in the last sentence!

"We do not necessarily conquer through brilliance. We conquer by continuing."

Take action on the challenges you face. The moment you become aware of your source of discouragement, get busy working on a solution. Nothing will take away your discouragement more quickly than taking positive steps to overcome the challenge.

Remember, God's delays are not necessarily God's denials. Many times what appears impossible in the short term becomes very possible in the long run, *if you persist along his path for you.* When the going gets tough, I'm tempted to quit just like the next person. The key to success is continuing to take steps toward your goal even when it's difficult and you don't feel like keepin' on.

I couldn't help but crack a smile when I stumbled across and read a copy of 'The Possibility Thinkers' Creed:'

"When faced with a mountain I will not quit, I will keep on striving until I climb over, find a pass through, tunnel underneath or simply stay and turn the mountain into a gold mine, with God's help."

Wally Amos, founder of Famous Amos Cookies, recently told a reporter interviewing him that Robert Schuller had tremendously affected his life with this statement: "The three important things are: Faith, focus and follow through — and fulfillment follows those three." I've pondered these words many times and they have also impacted my life. First off, it takes faith in your vision, dreams, goals and especially in God who gave them to you. The next step is to lock on to your dreams by focusing your energy, brain power and emotion on the desired result. Third, if you want your dreams to come true you must follow through with actions that are in alignment with your faith and focus. The book of Ecclesiastes states, "Whatever your hand finds to do, do it with all your might."

"That which we persist in doing becomes easier for us to do; not that the nature of the thing itself is changed, but that our power to do is increased."
— Ralph Waldo Emerson

"If you encounter difficulty, don't change your decision to go. Change your direction to get there."

Abundant Life is a Risky Adventure

Five frogs are sitting on a log and one decides he is going to jump. How many frogs would be left on the log? Four? No! Five would be left. Deciding to jump is not the same as jumping!

This poem by Leo Buscaglia has much to say concerning the element of risk:

"Life is either a daring adventure or nothing."
— Helen Keller

"To laugh is to risk appearing the fool.
To weep is to risk appearing sentimental.
To reach out for another is to risk involvement.
To expose feeling is to risk exposing your true self.
To place your ideas, your dreams, before the crowd is to risk being called naive.
To love is to risk not being loved in return.
To live is to risk dying.
To hope is to risk despair.
To try is to risk failure.
But risks must be taken, because the greatest risk in life is to risk nothing. The person who risks nothing, does nothing, has nothing and is nothing and becomes nothing. He may avoid suffering and sorrow, but he simply cannot learn and feel and change and grow and love, and live. Chained by his certitudes, he's a slave. He's forfeited his freedom. Only the person who risks is truly free."

"Go ahead and take the risk. Climb out on a limb from the tree of life — that's where the fruit is!"
— Kevin Baerg

Without risk, no faith is necessary and without faith, we know it's impossible to please God. Greg Peterson says, "Living by faith is risky business!" However, our faith is not in man or in something fashioned with our own hands. Our faith is in the living God, the Creator of the entire universe! I feel a whole lot more comfortable taking risks with God on my side than taking them on my own.

Excellence can be attained if you...
Care more than others think is wise.
Risk more than others think is safe.
Dream more than others think is practical.
Expect more than others think is possible.

Make a Difference

"Behold the turtle: he makes progress only when he sticks his neck out."
— James Bryant Conant

In Maine they tell of an old man walking along the beach with his grandson, who picked up each starfish they passed and tenderly threw it back into the sea. "If I leave them up here," the little boy said, "they will dry up and die. I'm saving their lives."

"But," protested the old man, "the beach goes on for miles, and there are millions of starfish. What you are doing won't make any difference."

"Act as if what you do makes a difference. It does.
— William James

The boy looked at the starfish in his hand, gently threw it back into the ocean, and answered softly, "It will make a difference to this one."

People want to make a difference with their life. Taking action on your God-given dreams will ensure that your life counts, even though it may not look like it at times. God is the one keeping the score!

If You Want It Bad Enough

"If you want a thing bad enough
To go out and fight for it
To work day and night for it
To give up your time, your peace
And your sleep for it
If all that you dream
And you scheme is about it
And life is useless
And worthless without it,
If you'd gladly sweat for it

"Concerning all acts of initiative and creation, there is one elementary truth — that the moment one definitely commits oneself, then Providence moves, too."
— Goethe

And fret for it and plan for it
And lose all your terror
Of the opposition for it,
If you go after it
With all your capacity,
Your strength and sagacity,
Faith hope and confidence
And stern pertinacity,
If neither cold, poverty,
Famine nor gulf,
Sickness nor pain of body or brain,
Can keep you away from the thing that you want,
If dogged and grim
You besiege and beset it,
With the help of God,
You'll get it!"
— Author Unknown

"Knowing what
your goal is and
desiring to reach it
doesn't bring you
closer to it. Doing
something does."
— George Eld

Steps to Developing a Plan of Action

1. Clearly determine what it is you want to achieve. Establish an exciting goal.
2. How important is achieving your goal? Get leverage on yourself by answering these two questions:
   a. What will you miss out on if you don't reach this goal? What pain will you experience as a result of not accomplishing it?
   b. What great things will happen as a result of reaching this goal? What joy and pleasure will it bring into your life because you accomplished it?
3. Write out a faith reminder that clearly pictures the attainment of your goal with all the positive emotion that goes with it.
4. Do you foresee any obstacles in your path? Why haven't you achieved the goal before?
5. What are the solutions to the obstacles?

*"Somebody should
tell us, right at the
start of our lives,
that we are dying.
Then we might live
life to the limit,
every minute of
every day. Do it! I
say. Whatever you
want to do, do it
now! There are
only so many
tomorrows."*
— Michael Landon

6. What actions can you take to bring the solution to pass? Transfer these actions to your daily planner on the appropriate date.
7. Set an evaluation date for each action item.
8. Write out faith reminders for each solution to the obstacles.

Remember, 45% of the subconscious impact of a faith reminder is brought on by developing a vividly clear picture in your mind. Another 45% is wrapped up in the emotions and feelings that accompany the imagined, accomplished goal. *Only 10% is produced by reading the words by themselves.*

By assimilating your goals into your subconscious (using your faith reminders) you are developing belief without evidence that will generate motivation and desire.

"Obstacles are those frightful things you see when you take your eyes off your goal."
—Henry Ford

Personal Application:

Review the lifetime goals you wrote in the last chapter. Identify the top five you would most like to take action on at this time. Now choose one of the five and develop an action plan for it. Follow the steps outlined above to fill out an Action Plan Worksheet for your exciting goal! Look over the completed Action Plan Worksheet on pages 188-189.

You may wish to transfer your goal, the solutions and your faith reminders to the front and back of a 3 x 5 card or your daily planner so you can refer to it often. (For additional blank forms, visit www.inspiration4u.com).

"Commit to the Lord whatever you do, and your plans will succeed."
— Proverbs

Action Plan

My Goal:

What will I miss out on if I don't reach this goal?

What great things will happen as a result of reaching this goal?

Obstacle	Solutions

Obstacle	Solutions

Obstacle	Solutions

Worksheet

Today's Date: _____

Target Completion: _____

My Goal Faith Reminder:

Actual Completion: _____

_____

_____

My Solution Faith Reminders:

Action Item		Eval. Date/Transfer Date		

Action Item		Eval. Date/Transfer Date		

Action Item		Eval. Date/Transfer Date		

"Only begin and then the mind grows heated; only begin and the task will be completed."
— Goethe

Maximize Your Resources
— *Taking Control of Your Time and Treasure*

"He who is faithful in a very little thing is faithful also in much; and he who is unfaithful in a very little thing is also unfaithful in much."

— Jesus

God wants us to be good stewards of our time and money. This chapter will give you principles you can use to better manage and prioritize your time and finances. Fulfilling your dreams will require that you have a system set in place to control these vital resources.

"Lack of resources is not our problem. It is lack of resourcefulness."
— Billy Ray Cox

Part 1: Taking Control of Your Time

We know we are supposed to make the most of our time, because time is precious — it is limited — we all have only 24 hours each day. *No one gets even one tiny minute more than anybody else!*

Here, the famous words of William Penn are applicable, though they were written almost three hundred years ago. "There is nothing of which we are apt to be so lavish of as time, and about which we ought to be more solicitous, since without it we can do nothing in this world. Time is what we want most, but what, alas! we use worst, and for which God will certainly most strictly reckon with us, when time shall be no more."

It would be a huge presumption for me to think that in half a chapter I can share all you need to know about time management.

However, I do want to quickly cover some of the insight I've gathered over the years. I am a sucker for every new time management course or system that comes along. I'm always looking for new and better ways to get more of the right things done in less time.

Examine Your Life

"Teach us to number our days aright, that we might gain a heart of wisdom."
— Psalms

Your destination is more important than how fast you're moving. Life can be so hectic with, phone calls, paper work, bills, meetings and other scheduled events. People feel as if they're running everywhere — pushed to the limit.

We do a lot of things, but are we doing what really counts?

A child's father kept bringing home office work just about every night. Finally his son in the first grade asked him why.

His dad said, "Son, I simply have more work to do than I can finish during the day."

The boy responded, "Well Daddy, why don't they put you in a slower group?"

We always hear about the fast track in life. Perhaps it is high time some of us considered the slow track! We are constantly faced with making choices about how we spend our time, from the major issues to the small details in life. We also get to live with the results of those choices, and many of us don't like the consequences — especially when we see a gap between what we spend our time on and what is truly important.

Using the system I am about to show you will help you to close this gap and get you to truly focus on high value activities.

Created to Win!
Time Management Grid

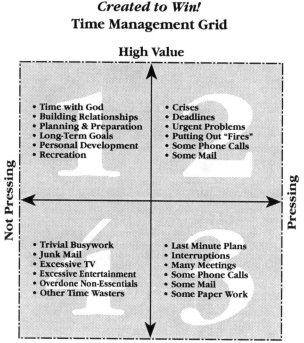

High Value

Not Pressing / **Pressing**

Section 1:
• Time with God
• Building Relationships
• Planning & Preparation
• Long-Term Goals
• Personal Development
• Recreation

Section 2:
• Crises
• Deadlines
• Urgent Problems
• Putting Out "Fires"
• Some Phone Calls
• Some Mail

Section 4:
• Trivial Busywork
• Junk Mail
• Excessive TV
• Excessive Entertainment
• Overdone Non-Essentials
• Other Time Wasters

Section 3:
• Last Minute Plans
• Interruptions
• Many Meetings
• Some Phone Calls
• Some Mail
• Some Paper Work

Low Value

A key principle of effective life management is the Created to Win! Time Management Grid. It separates activities that have high value from those with low value. It determines how pressing or urgent they are. With these criteria, activities can be organized into four basic categories:

- Section 1 activities are not pressing, yet have the highest value.
- Section 2 activities are pressing and have high value.
- Section 3 activities are pressing but have low value.
- Section 4 activities are not pressing and have the lowest value.

We tend to devote time and attention to things in an inverse relation to their importance.

> *"Doing things right is not as important as doing the right things!"*
> — Peter Drucker

Where do you spend the bulk of your time? Most of us spend much of our time in sections 2 and 3. If you were a chronic section 4 person, you wouldn't be reading this book. Where do you want to focus more of your time and energy? If you will spend more of your 'best' time in section 1, many of the crisis's and 'fires' in section 2 wouldn't even happen. You could empower others to handle your section 3's and have the strength to avoid the section 4's!

Not More Things — Different things

Many of us need to do different things, not just more things. Instead of prioritizing the proverbial 'to-do' list, I encourage you to step back, examine what's really important to you and block out some time for it. Rather than wondering whether you have enough time to get all the things on your to-do list done, how about scheduling your top priorities? This way you can put your values ahead of the clock in your life.

"It's not so much how busy you are, but why you are busy. The bee is praised. The mosquito is swatted."
— Marie O'Connor

You will also find looking at the week as a whole instead of just focusing on one day enables you to make better decisions as you schedule your high value activities. Reviewing your vision, mission, values and goals before planning your week helps you decide where to place an activity or whether it should be done at all.

"Will what I'm planning on doing move me towards the fulfillment of my goals in alignment with my values?" This is the question you want to ask yourself on a daily basis.

Organizing Your Time

The following time management process I've outlined empowers you to shift your focus from

urgency to value and from efficiency to
effectiveness:

1. Review your vision, personal mission
   statement, your values and your top goals.
   This provides the framework for your
   decisions.
2. Identify or review your key roles and
   relationships. This enables you to plan
   with a balanced view of the entire scope
   of your life.
3. Select Section 1 goals for each role. These
   are goals that will help you achieve the
   things that have extremely high value to
   you. These goals are usually very
   important, but not very urgent.
4. Take a week-at-a-glance perspective and
   block out time for these high-leverage
   goals. Don't leave their accomplishment to
   chance. Carve out time for your priorities.
   ***For a free weekly planner template, please call
   1-800-539-2350 or visit www.inspiration4u.com***
5. For each day, list all of the other action
   items you choose to work on, recognizing
   that some of these may be section 2 items.
6. Use a journal or notes section to record
   important thoughts, notes, decisions and
   actions. This becomes part of your
   personal reference library.

> *"The future is
> something which
> everyone reaches at
> the rate of sixty
> minutes an hour,
> whatever they do,
> whoever they are."*
> — C.S. Lewis

Some of you may feel that life allows you
very little discretionary time. You just don't
seem to get time in very large chunks. Perhaps
you too will get some encouragement from this
story out of Daily Family Devotions:

"A devout Amish woman once said, 'I seem
to create so much of my life the way I fashion
my rugs — from leftover remnants and tatters of
whole days.' How seldom we have days that are
in 'one piece,' unmarred by intrusions and

interruptions. We find ourselves having to take a sliver of time here to read a story to our child, a scrap of a moment there to make a call . . . another ragged piece of an hour to mow the lawn or hem a dress . . . a discarded handful of minutes to write a note. Yet when we take them all, and dye them in the bright colors of our love, sew them together with the strong cord of devotion, and plait them faithfully through the weeks, what delightful, beautiful things have been fashioned! Never be defeated by a day which seems to be nothing but bits and tatters. Use each precious moment for needs as they come rather than waiting for 'whole pieces of cloth,' and whole uninterrupted days, for they may never come."

"The best thing about the future is that it comes only one day at a time."
— Abraham Lincoln

Take Time

Take time to think. . . It is the source of power.
Take time to play. . . It is the secret of perpetual youth.
Take time to read. . . It is the fountain of wisdom.
Take time to pray. . . It is the greatest power on earth.
Take time to love and be loved. . . It is a God-given privilege.
Take time to be friendly. . . It is the road to happiness.
Take time to laugh. . . It is the music of the soul.
Take time to give. . . It is too short a day to be selfish.
Take time to work. . . It is the price of success.

These are the Good Ol' Days

A father tells this heart warming story about a lesson he learned from his son.

"School had just closed for the summer. My son came in, flung his books to a corner of the room where they'd rest for two months, and asked in an excited voice, 'Dad, can you take me to the swimming pool?'

I answered, 'Yes, in about five minutes. Hurry, I've got an appointment.'

He bounced down the steps, grabbed a towel, threw it around his neck, and headed for the car. On his way, he stopped abruptly, opened wide his arms as if to embrace the world, and said, 'Now Dad, for the good ol' days!'

As he ran to the car I didn't run with him, but stood there thinking for a few pensive moments. Most people *look back* on their lives and say, 'Those were the good ol' days,' but not my twelve-year-old. He wasn't looking back nor ahead but *only at the present*, the moment of now.

He was right, was he not? The present — this moment — now — is all we actually have. These are good days — good old days, good new days, just good days, period. These are days in which our best energies are demanded, our finest talents called for, and our most expert management of time required."

I like that approach to life! If the good ol' days are all behind us, what does the future hold? If the best has already passed us by, how are we going to get excited about today? Today is the best day of your life because it is in your grasp right now! Only God knows what tomorrow might bring. Let's *make* our days great by being equal to the opportunities at hand.

"Go, eat your food with gladness, and drink your wine with a joyful heart, for it is now that God favors what you do."
— Ecclesiastes

"Yesterday is past. Tomorrow is a dream. Today is a gift — that's why we call it 'the present.'"

If I Had My Life to Live Over

"Did you ever hear of a person who had striven all their life faithfully and singly toward an object and in no measure obtained it? If a person constantly aspires, are they not elevated?"

— Henry David Thoreau

I'd dare to make more mistakes next time.
I'd relax — I would limber up.
I would be sillier than I have been this trip.
I would take fewer things seriously.
I would take more chances.
I would take more trips.
I would climb more mountains and swim more rivers.
I would eat more ice cream and less beans.
I would perhaps have more actual troubles but I'd have fewer imaginary ones.
You see, I'm one of those people who live sensibly and sanely hour after hour, day after day.
Oh, I've had my moments, and if I had it to do over again, I'd have more of them. In fact, I'd try to do nothing else. Just moments.
One after the other, instead of living so many years ahead of each day.
I've been one of those persons who never go anywhere without a thermometer, a hot water bottle, a rain coat and a parachute.
If I had to do it again, I would travel lighter next time.
If I had my life to live over,
I would start barefoot earlier in the spring, and stay that way later in the fall.
I would go to more dances.
I would ride more merry-go-rounds.
I would pick more daisies.
— Nadine Stair (age 85)

What you do today is very important, because you're exchanging a day of your life for it.

Personal Application:

Review the Time Management Grid on page 157. Think about all the different activities that you give your time to. In which section do they fall? Take a few moments to write down the activities you do on a regular basis in the appropriate section. Then estimate the amount of time you spend in each area on an average day.

• Section 1 — Not pressing/Highest value.

_____

_____

_____

• Section 2 — Pressing/High value.

_____

_____

_____

• Section 3 — Not pressing/Low value.

_____

_____

_____

• Section 4 — Not pressing/Lowest value.

_____

_____

_____

"Resolved, to live with all my might while I do live. Resolved, never to lose one moment of time, to improve it in the most profitable way I possibly can. Resolved, never to do anything which I should despise or think meanly of in another. Resolved, never to do anything out of revenge. Resolved, never to do anything which I should be afraid to do if it were the last hour of my life."
— Jonathan Edwards

Part 2: Taking Control of Your Treasure

Money — hard to live with it, but you can't live without it! Money is so important that Jesus spent more time talking about financial issues than almost any other topic. *Money isn't the most important thing in life, but it's right up there with oxygen!*

"Make money your god and it will plague you like the devil."
— Henry Fielding

Some people try to pretend that money doesn't matter, but financial pressure is something that affects most of us everyday of our lives. A lack of money often translates into a lack of important resources — especially for those with fixed incomes and in many cases, single income families. With a lack of money, we will find it very difficult to fulfill many of our dreams and goals.

Is money the agent that fulfills our dreams or is it the root of all evil? The scripture does say "the *love* of money is **a** root of all kinds (not every kind) of evil" but **money itself is neutral.** *It is only our attitude toward money and what we do with it that makes it good or evil.* It is merely a medium of exchange — a means to an end.

Many people make the mistake of thinking all their problems would go away with enough money. This is not true. Money in and of itself does not solve life's challenges. Equally untrue is the notion that greater financial freedom and abundance would not open more doors for you to grow, share and invest in your life and in the lives of those around you.

How is it in this land of incredible economic opportunity, that 95 percent of the American people, by the age of sixty-five, after working their entire life, are unable to support themselves without assistance from the government or family? I believe there are several reasons:

Why So Few Live in Abundance:

1. **People have mixed associations** linked to what it takes to make more money and what it means to have an abundance. We send mixed signals to our brain and therefore reap mixed results. We know that money can provide us with a degree of freedom, opportunities to give, and the chance to do the things we really enjoy. However, simultaneously we may also believe that in order to make this extra money we would have to work too hard and too long to really enjoy it. We may have a type of money phobia, like many people do, and believe that too much money makes you less spiritual, and that a poverty mentality is what God desires. We may also resent other people's success, which subconsciously sends the message to our minds that having extra money is bad. Our brain interprets this in such a way that we begin to believe that being wealthy makes us a bad person. In order to build an abundance we need to change these negative associations.

   "A wise fellow should have money in his head, but not in his heart."
   — Jonathan Swift

2. **People think finances are too complex**, that they need an expert to help them and so they basically do nothing about it. Having an expert give you tips on how you can increase your effectiveness is always a welcome proposition. Although, once you understand the fundamentals you'll discover that managing your money is a fairly straightforward and simple matter.

3. **People tend to have a scarcity mentality.** They live in a world where everything is limited: only so much time, so many opportunities, so much available land, so much oil, or so many homes. They believe that in order to win, somebody has to lose. That is not necessarily true. Technology has radically changed our life-styles and today it determines the value of a physical resource, not how large the supply of it is. Take oil for example; in 1973 during the gas shortage, the best experts in the world estimated that we had only 700 billion barrels of oil left in the world. Now, over 20 years of consumption later, supply estimates are as high as 3000 billion barrels! What happened? Technology enabled us to find more oil and utilize it more efficiently. Fuel injectors alone have saved millions of barrels of oil. God truly has given us an abundance of everything we need and the creative brain power to properly manage and best utilize these resources.

"Our cup will truly run over only after we have sealed the character cracks."
— John D. Rockefeller

How Can You Get in on the Abundance?

Increase Your Value

The number one way to earn more income and create more abundance in your life is to **become more valuable**. Develop more skills, more ability, more specialized knowledge, a greater capacity to do what others aren't willing to do. This allows you to *add more real value to people's lives.* Why is a doctor paid more than a stock boy? The doctor adds more value to the lives of those he or she comes in contact with. Most anyone can become a stock boy rather quickly, but to become a doctor takes years of preparation and development.

The real purpose of any business is to create and deliver products and services that directly increase the quality of life for all the customers they serve. If a business consistently does this for a significant number of people, then producing a profit is virtually assured.

"What if I'm not an entrepreneur?" You ask. You don't have to be one to add more value to what you do. Seek to continually grow and expand in your knowledge, skills and your attitudes in order to give more. The way to earn more money where you are planted today is to ask yourself (and perhaps your boss), *"How can I be worth more to this company?"* "How can I help it to achieve more with less?" "How can I help increase the quality of its products and services while at the same time, cut costs?" "What new ideas or suggestions can I produce that would really make a difference?" "How much money can I make or save my organization this year?"

"When you do more than you're paid to do, you'll eventually be paid more for what you do."
— Zig Ziglar

Honor God First.

Even the secular world talks about the power of giving and tithing. Tithing means simply giving one tenth of our income to the work of God. The book of Malachi tells us to test God in only one thing, "'Bring the whole tithe into the storehouse, that there may be food in my house. Test me in this,' says the Lord Almighty, 'and see if I will not throw open the floodgates of heaven and pour out so much blessing that you will not have room enough for it. I will prevent pests from devouring your crops, and the vines in your fields will not cast their fruit.'" Some have suggested that the 'pests' referred to in the preceding verse are modern day Internal Revenue Service agents!

Another benefit from tithing is that by giving away a portion of what you earn, even when you don't have everything you need or want, you teach your mind that you have more than enough. You're beyond scarcity and that new belief alone will have an incredible impact on your life. The book of Proverbs tells us to "Honor the Lord with your wealth, with the firstfruits of all your crops; then your barns will be filled to overflowing, and your vats will brim over with new wine."

Invest in Your Future

"The average family's ambition is to make as much money as they're spending."

There is only one way to accumulate and maintain wealth, however this way is extremely unpopular today. **Spend less than you earn and invest the difference**. Not very complicated is it? It is the only way to have an abundance in the long run. No matter how much money people earn, they somehow find ways to spend it. There are people who are just as strapped as we might feel that earn 6 and 7 figure incomes. *It's not how much you make, but how much you save* — that's the key.

A friend was trying to encourage his elderly mother to enjoy the money she had accumulated through her frugal living. "Mother," he said, "you have enough money to last you until you're a hundred."

"And then what will I do?" She replied.

The best way to increase your savings (or begin it as the case may be) is to choose a specific percentage of your income that you will invest and have it come right out of your paycheck or bank account. "But I can't save 10% of my income right now?" Who said we all have to start at 10%? How about 1% or 2% to start? A little bit invested consistently over the long haul can really grow thanks to the wonder of compound interest. Like the proverb says, "He who gathers money little by little makes it grow."

Develop a Spending Plan *(rather than a budget)*

How's that for using positive vocabulary? Your spending plan is a tool. You decide what you want to spend money on in advance, rather than being caught up in a spur of the moment decision. Many times that impulsive decision leads to a purchase you later regret. Most Americans live far beyond their means. The amount of credit card debt has more than tripled over the last 10 years. Too much consumer debt practically guarantees financial disaster. Avoid the credit trap!

"Budgeting is a method of worrying before you spend rather than afterward."
— Anonymous

If you're married, another benefit of establishing a monthly spending plan for each category is it can save a lot of arguments. Once you've established your spending plan, keep track of how you're doing. What use is your plan if you don't consistently measure your progress?

Keep in mind the parable of the talents. The bottom line is that God wants us to be faithful and wise with the finances he gives us. If you don't use it right, you lose it. Jesus said, "For everyone who has will be given more, and he will have an abundance. Whoever does not have, even what he has will be taken from him." In other words, if you're a good steward, God will entrust you with more. If you aren't faithful, even the little that you have will be taken from you and given to the one who is faithful. It sure doesn't sound like communism to me!

"Ere you consult your fancy, consult your purse."
— Benjamin Franklin

In everyday reality, money tends to flow

away from those who don't manage it well, into the hands of those who do. It's that simple.

Seek God for His Increase

Our incredible Heavenly Father loves to give us wonderful things and bless us with a full life. He's 'El Shaddai,' not El Cheapo! The God who is more than enough, not the God who just gets by. We need to break out of the 'break-even' comfort zone. The prophet Isaiah says there is no end to God's increase. Don't set your heart on breaking even, set it on increase. Don't just aim to get out of debt (being behind) but to get ahead, to increase, to prosper. Why? In order to give, contribute and invest!

"God be gracious to us and bless us, and cause His face to shine upon us. That Thy way may be known on the earth, Thy salvation among all nations." This Psalm was the theme verse on Patty's and my wedding invitation and has always been our heart cry. *May God bless us so we can be a blessing to others.*

How are we going to positively influence the world for God if we're not increasing our resources? Where in the scriptures is it written, "Embrace living for God, where life is less filling and has only one third of the blessings you can get from selfish living?"

From the very beginning, God's plan for us was to be happy and prosperous. Except for the fruit of the one tree, he gave everything on the planet to Adam and Eve. They were the richest people in history — after all, they had all the oil! What happened? Instead of living with an attitude of gratitude for all their blessings, they chose to focus on the one thing they didn't have and lust after it. We often fall into the same trap. I personally believe that If mankind had not

"You can have everything in life that you want if you simply help enough other people get what they want."
— Zig Ziglar

"There's a vast difference between standard of living and quality of life."

fallen, we'd still be in the garden enjoying the completely full life God originally planned for us.

God knows each of our hearts and, from his experience with mankind since the beginning, he knows how easy it is for us to forget him when we have abundance. Therefore he is careful not to give us more than we can bear and risk our relationship with him. When we're faithful with the little and keep God first in our lives, he knows he can entrust us with more.

"But remember the Lord your God, for it is he who gives you the ability to produce wealth."
— Moses

Enjoy the Wealth God has Given You

God loves to bless his children, but like us when we give, he appreciates a grateful, thankful response. Do you realize that just living in America or Canada gives you and me incredible wealth. Think of all the benefits; incredible road systems, extensive libraries, free education, gorgeous parks, clean water, freedom of expression, freedom of religion and the freedom to vote. We are already thoroughly blessed! Let's be grateful and learn to enjoy all the abundance we have in our life right this moment. Remember to thank God in particular for his love for you and also for your relationships with your families and friends.

In an interview with John M. Templeton, he said that faith is our soundest resource. Templeton is a top Wall Street money manager, a multimillionaire and founder of the world's largest prize for achievement, the "Templeton Prize for Progress in Religion."

"Trust in God magnifies our life." He said. "It enlarges our perspective beyond surface appearances and beyond our own smallness and limitations. It also makes for a pervasive sense of gratitude for the blessings of everyday existence, and that gratitude in turn flows out in

"The blessing of the Lord brings wealth, and he adds no trouble to it."
— Proverbs

efforts to help others. If you are seeking wholeheartedly to help other people, you cannot prevent rewards coming back to you in terms of friendship, love, and esteem."

He added, "Happiness comes to those who try to give happiness to others. You cannot get happiness by seeking it, but only by trying to give it away."

"Not he who has much is rich, but he who gives much."
— Erich Fromm

In the early 1990's, Templeton managed $18 billion in 81 investment funds for 800,000 individual investors, numerous universities and pension funds. He tithes 10 percent of his own income to religious and charitable causes. Yet, from scanty beginnings, he has become an enormously wealthy man, giving away more than $1 million annually. He's also recognized in financial circles as one of Wall Street's keenest market analysts.

"In all my lifetime of helping thousands of people, almost every person I've known who tithed for as long as 10 years has become both prosperous and happy."

The Balance of Contentment

As in anything else, there is a balance when it comes to wealth. It is certainly easier to go to either extreme: Chasing after riches or taking a vow of poverty. However, the book of Ecclesiastes states, "It is good to grasp the one and not let go of the other. The man who respects God will avoid all extremes." We're talking about that elusive 'radical middle' again! May God help each of us to find it.

The collection of verses that follow might challenge your thinking and hopefully help you gain an even healthier perspective on the accumulation of wealth.

"Do not wear yourself out to get rich; have

the wisdom to show restraint. Cast but a glance at riches, and they are gone, for they will surely sprout wings and fly off to the sky like an eagle"
— *Proverbs*

"Better one handful with tranquillity than two handfuls with toil and chasing after wind"
— *Ecclesiastes*

"Whoever loves money never has enough; whoever loves wealth is never satisfied with his income"
— *Ecclesiastes*

"Moreover, when God gives any man wealth and possessions, and enables him to enjoy them, to accept his lot and be happy in his work — this is a gift of God. He seldom reflects on the days of his life, because God keeps him occupied with gladness of heart"
— *Ecclesiastes*

"My problem lies in reconciling my gross habits with my net income."
— Errol Flynn

Pretty incredible words aren't they? It's amazing that these pearls of wisdom, of which some are well over 2000 years old, can be so relevant today!

Personal Application:

What actions are you going to take to change your financial situation? Write them out in the space below:

_____

_____

_____

_____

_____

_____

"You can have more than you've got when you become more than you are."
— Zig Ziglar

_____

_____

_____

_____

_____

_____

_____

The Key to Lasting Happiness
— *Building Loving Relationships*

"And now these three remain: faith,
hope, and love. But the greatest of these
is love."

— *St. Paul*

Everyone has been created to have relationships, first with God and then with others. If you aren't in right relationship with God and those around you — watch out! It will negatively affect every area of your life. Without healthy relationships you will never find true success or obtain lasting happiness. In this chapter I hope to encourage you to make all your relationships great, filled with the true love from above.

"How happy you are depends to a very large degree on your relationships with other people."
— Zig Ziglar

One of my favorite Peanuts cartoons shows Charlie Brown and Linus having one of their frequent philosophical discussions. Charlie Brown asks, "Do you ever think much about the future, Linus?"

Linus responds, "Oh, yes . . . all the time."

Charlie Brown turns to Linus and asks, "What do you think you'd like to be when you grow up?"

In the last frame Linus responds:
"Outrageously happy!"

I like that goal. Outrageous happiness. That's also a pretty good description of Heaven! How can we be outrageously happy on earth? By having outrageously wonderful relationships!

No matter how much 'stuff' we accumulate or what level of achievement we reach, life is fairly miserable without someone to share it all with. Now that doesn't necessarily mean a marriage partner, it can be any close relationship. After all, it is the relationships we have in life that bring us those 'Kodak' moments.

I like Emerson's definition of success:

Success:

"Someday, I hope to enjoy enough of what the world calls success so that if somebody asks me, 'What's the secret of it?' I shall say this: 'I get up when I fall down.'"
— Paul Harvey

"To laugh often and much;
to win the respect of intelligent people
and the affection of children;
to earn the appreciation of honest critics
and endure the betrayal of false friends;
to appreciate beauty,
to find the best in others;
to leave the world a bit better, whether by a
*   healthy child,*
a garden patch or a redeemed social
*   condition;*
to know even one life has breathed easier
*   because you have lived.*
This is to have succeeded."
— *Ralph Waldo Emerson*

Your Relationship with God

This is your most vital relationship and it is also the foundation for every area of your existence. I can't even imagine living without my relationship with God! He is the strength of my life and the source of my power. He is my Savior and Lord. He is the author and perfecter of my faith and the lover of my soul. If you don't have a relationship with God, I invite you to start one right now. Allow God to be involved in every area of your life.

If this is something you've already experienced before, but God has not been in the forefront of your life lately, I urge you to renew this crucial relationship. Give him your all! He won't let you down. He'll meet you right where you are and take you on from there. God longs to be *first in your life.*

How can you improve your relationship with the living God? The same way you grow any relationship, *by spending quality time* with him. Here are some ways you can enjoy his presence:

- Read the scriptures
- Prayer (talking *and* listening)
- Praise and worship (by yourself or with a group)

In reality, you can experience the presence of God anytime and anywhere you go. Know he is with you wherever you are. God truly is "the friend who sticks closer than a brother."

> *For a free audiocassette sharing how I developed a personal relationship with God, "Dare to Dream Again," please call 1-800-539-2350 or visit www.inspiration4u.com*

Your Relationship with Your Spouse

For those of you who are married, the second most important relationship you have is with your spouse. God has always intended for the two of you to be a team and work together. Your spouse should be your best friend. If they aren't, your marriage will show it. Best friends stick together no matter what. Best friends share their heart with each other — they talk about virtually everything. Sometimes it only takes a glance, or a brief clue to communicate with one another.

"If you treat your wife like a thoroughbred, you'll never end up with a nag."
— Zig Ziglar

However, sometimes the communication shorthand doesn't work exactly as expected. A wife was planning to have duck for dinner and so she hung a reminder to herself and pinned it with a magnet to the refrigerator — it read, cryptically, "Thaw Duck." The next day her husband saw the note and added his comment to it, "Thaw one, too."

For those of you whose spouse *is* their best friend, you know what I'm talking about. My wife, Patty and I truly are best friends and we can hardly get enough time together. If this isn't where you are at right now, don't despair. God can bring you together and help you attain the level of intimacy you desire. The most important thing you can do is spend time doing fun things together. Think back to your time of dating and all the crazy things you did. Get back in that 'courting' mode, loosen up and have some fun — **together!** I am convinced that if couples spent half the time and effort toward staying together as they expended in courting each other, the divorce rate would plummet!

"Real love is when you do the things that are best for the person you love."

An article by Dr. Joyce Brothers prescribes the morning kiss as the secret to long life and success: "A group of German psychologists, physicians and insurance companies cooperated on a research project and found, according to Dr. Arthur Sazbo of West Germany, that the key to longer, happier, healthier and wealthier lives for men lies in one single act. All you have to do is. . .kiss your wife each morning when you leave for work! You don't have to feel like kissing her; just do it. The meticulous German researchers discovered that men who kiss their wives every morning have fewer automobile accidents on their way to work than men who omit the morning kiss. The good-morning kissers miss less work because of sickness than the non-kissers. And they earn 20 to 30 percent more money and live some five years longer than men who are stingy with their kisses". I imagine that this approach would prove equally effective for a woman kissing her husband before she leaves for work.

Willard F. Harley, Jr. has written an incredible book entitled, "His Needs, Her Needs," that tells how to 'affair proof' your marriage. In it he identifies the ten most important marital needs of husbands and wives and teaches you how to fulfill them. Of these top ten needs, men and women each have five, however they are all interrelated.

His Needs:
- Sexual Fulfillment
- Recreational Companionship
- An Attractive Spouse
- Domestic Support
- Admiration

Her Needs:
- Affection
- Conversation
- Honesty and Openness
- Financial Support
- Family Commitment

Harley goes so far as to say that even if you meet four out of the five needs, you still leave the relationship open to a possible affair. Patty and I have gone over this book together and we heartily agree with him. I urge every couple to get a copy and take a weekend to read it together. Make sure that you go through the questions at the end of each chapter, and talk about everything with absolute transparency. If you've got a great marriage, it will help you keep it that way. If your marriage is on the other end of the spectrum, it just might save it.

"Successful marriages require skill — skill in caring for the one you promised to cherish throughout life. Good intentions are not enough."
— Willard F. Harley

Your Relationship with Your Children

"Behold, children are a gift of the Lord; the fruit of the womb is a reward." — Psalms

Your relationship with your children comes a

very close third in priority after your spouse. Children definitely are a gift from the Lord — a precious blessing from his hand to yours! Once again, the key ingredient in these relationships is time together. Our kids grow up so fast and before you know it they're on their own. It's hard to believe that I probably only have 5-7 years left with my precious children at home (possibly only 2 with Sarah just finishing up 10th grade). I want to make those years count!

"Now is the time to love. Tomorrow the baby won't need to be rocked, the toddler won't be asking, "Why?" The schoolboy won't need help with his lessons, nor will he bring his school friends home for some fun. Tomorrow the teenager will have made his major decisions."
— John Dresches

Two women, riding the subway together, were discussing their children and the difficulties of raising a family. They talked about needing new clothes and shoes, how expensive it was to feed them, and how difficult it was to keep the children in spending money. On and on the complaining went. A woman sitting in front of them turned around and interrupted them. "I couldn't help but overhear you. I used to be like that, but no more. Our son was a great expense to us and we had to sacrifice to give him what he needed." She paused as her eyes brimmed with tears. "But then he died. Now he doesn't cost us a cent. Oh, I would give the world to have him back again."

It's so easy to get caught up in the busyness of life and lose proper perspective. We tend to become frustrated by things that are actually blessings in disguise. How hard it is some days to tell the difference.

Gary Smalley says the secret of close-knit families is growing through crisis situations together. The bonding doesn't show in the middle of the crisis, but it is happening nonetheless and later on becomes a memory your family will never forget. One activity that consistently generates these crisis' is camping. It is one of the top common denominators researchers have found in successful, close-knit families. We love to camp as a family and every trip we've taken is a great memory — even with the downpours and challenging times. If you dislike camping, find something similar — but do spend time together! Make up a list of fun activities that you all would like to do and pick them off one by one.

"For a child, love is spelled T-I-M-E."

A family in the East was planning a month's vacation to the West Coast. At the last minute the father's work responsibilities prevented him from going, but the mother insisted she was capable of driving and that she and the kids would go ahead. Dad got out the maps and planned the route where the family should stop each night.

A couple of weeks later, the father completed his extra work responsibilities early. He decided to surprise the family, so he flew to a West Coast city without calling them. Then he took a taxi out into the country on a highway that, according to his travel plan, the family should be driving on later that day. The taxi driver dropped him off on the side of the road.

Dad waited there until he saw the family car coming, then stuck out his thumb as a 'hitch-hiker.' As Mom and the kids drove past, they did a double-take. One of the kids said, "Hey, wasn't that Dad?" Mom screeched to a stop, backed up to the 'hitch-hiker' and the family had a joyful reunion.

"Life is like playing a violin solo in public and learning the instrument as you go."
— Samuel Butler

Later, when a newspaper reporter asked the man why he would do such a crazy thing, he responded, "After I die, I want my kids to be able to say, 'Dad sure was fun wasn't he?'"

Your Relationship With Your Friends and Family

Quality friendships are wonderful to have, but they don't come easy. Love and sacrifice are prerequisite to a beautiful friendship.

Oliver Wendell Homes wrote: "There is no friend like an old friend who has shared our morning days, no greeting like his welcome, no homage like his praise."

All of us would like to have old friends. But have you ever stopped to think that old friends are not made in a hurry? If you would like to have such friends in the years to come, you had better start making new friends now. Sturdy friends, like sturdy beams, take time to season. Select people you feel pretty sure could be the kind of friends you would prize in later years. Then start the gentle, gradual seasoning process. How? Ralph Waldo Emerson gives the answer, "The only way to have a friend is to be a friend."

"A friend knows your weaknesses but shows you your strengths; feels your fears but fortifies your faith; sees your anxieties but frees your spirit; recognizes your disabilities but emphasizes your possibilities."
— William Arthur Ward

There were two friends who went backpacking into the wilderness. They woke up one morning and were standing by their tent having their first cup of coffee for the day. Suddenly, they spotted a grizzly bear heading toward them at full speed. Instantly, one man reached down and grabbed his tennis shoes and quickly started to put them on.

The other guy looked at him and said, "Are you crazy? What are you doing? Do you really think you can outrun that grizzly bear?"

His so-called friend said, "No, I don't need to. All I have to do is outrun you!"

When you have friends like this, you don't need any enemies! Walter Winchell said, "A real friend is one who walks in when the rest of the world walks out."

Friendships are important, but as the saying goes, 'blood is thicker than water.' Be careful not to get so involved with friends that you forget your extended family. God wants you to be a blessing to them. Look for the opportunities to do so!

A man stopped at a flower shop to order some flowers to be wired to his mother who lived two hundred miles away. As he got out of his car he noticed a young girl sitting on the curb sobbing. He asked her what was wrong and she replied: "I wanted to buy a red rose for my mother. But I only have 75 cents and a rose costs 2 dollars."

The man smiled and said, "Come on in with me. I'll buy you a rose." He bought the little girl her rose and ordered his own mother's flowers. As they were leaving he offered the girl a ride.

She said, "Yes, please! Take me to my mother." To his dismay, she directed him to a cemetery where she placed the rose on a freshly dug grave.

The man returned to the flower shop, canceled the wire order, picked up the flowers and drove two hundred miles to his mother's home.

In our busyness, we want to remember our parents and give back into their lives as well. It is all too easy to get caught up in our own life and neglect to spend time with our folks. Before you know it, the opportunity for special moments with them is gone.

"For a good self-image, choose your friends and your associates carefully."
— Zig Ziglar

"If you go out looking for friends, they're pretty scarce. If you go out to be a friend, you'll find them everywhere."

The Power of Love

"We can risk loving as passionately as God loves. For we know that the love God makes possible is no scarce resource that must be hoarded so that it can be distributed in dribs and drabs — a little here and a little there. Love is not a rare commodity; rather, the more we love with the intense particularity of God's love, the more we discover that we have the capacity to love." — *Stanley Hauerwas*

You can't 'outgive' God and you can't 'outlove' God. The more love you give out, the more love will multiply in your life. It isn't a dwindling resource. Love is as unlimited as God is. You can never run out as long as you remain plugged into the source.

"You are the salt of the earth, but remember, the world needs some sugar too."

A helpful way of looking at all our relationships is by remembering that everyone has a 'love bank.' This is a figure of speech describing a place inside of you that contains different accounts, one for each person you know. People make their deposits or withdrawals whenever we interact with them. Pleasurable interactions cause deposits, and painful interactions cause withdrawals. As life goes on, the accounts in our love bank fluctuate. Some of our acquaintances build sizable deposits. Some remain in the black, but have small balances. Still others go into the red because their accounts in our love bank are overdrawn.

It becomes very important as we grow in our marriage, and in all relationships for that matter, to keep the deposits going strong. This takes knowing the unique needs of the ones we love and seeking to meet those needs, without demanding something in return.

As you examine the relationships in your life, I want to encourage you to make sure each one of them is in good standing. If you need to forgive someone — do it and release them. If you need to be forgiven, remember to ask for forgiveness right away. Life is too short to let things come between us and the ones we love and care about. Let the healing power of God

flow through you into the lives of those around
you. Take time to strengthen the cords of love
that bind you together.

Anyway

*People are unreasonable, illogical and
    self-centered — love them anyway!
If you do good, people may accuse you of
    selfish ulterior motives — do good anyway!
If you are successful, you may win false
    friends and true enemies — succeed anyway!
The good you do today may be forgotten
    tomorrow — do good anyway!
Honesty and frankness make you vulnerable
    — be honest and frank anyway!
People favor underdogs but only follow top
    dogs — fight for some underdogs anyway!
What you spend building may be destroyed
    overnight — build anyway!
People really need help but may attack you if
    you help them — help them anyway!
Give the world the best you've got and you
    may get kicked in the teeth — give the world
    the best you've got anyway!*

Personal Application:

For one week (just to start) treat every person
you meet, without a single exception, as the
most important person on earth.

*You will find they will begin treating you the
very same way!*

A Personal Note

Thank you for taking this little journey of discovery with me. I am so excited about the prospect of you utilizing more of your God-given potential to reach your dreams!

If this book has helped or encouraged you, please take a moment and **tell** me about it. You can write a short note, send an e-mail to kevin@inspiration4u.com, call me at 1-800-539-2350 or leave a message in my AMVOX voicemail: 253-596-8077. You can also leave your review of this book at www.inspiration4u.com. *Your comments will help me know that my purpose and vision is being fulfilled.*

"Where you go from here is entirely up to you."

Robert Schuller tells this story. "When I was a little boy, I studied piano, and my mother was my teacher. When it came time for a recital, my mother made me go over the conclusion again and again. I had to get it down perfect! 'Keep on practicing the conclusion, Bob. Learn those last measures!' she used to say. 'Look, Bob, you can make a mistake in the beginning; or you can make a mistake in the middle; the people will forget it — if you make the ending glorious!'"

Make *your ending glorious!* I don't know all that has happened in your life. I don't even know where you are right now. But *I do know* that where you are today, God is present. Make God more a part of your life now, finish the race with him, and I can guarantee *your ending will be glorious!*

My prayer for you is that our gracious Heavenly Father will empower you to become the person he has always meant for you to be. May you fulfill all of his purposes for your life through the power of God living inside of you. May you achieve all the true success you could ever imagine and more!

Mission Statement Examples

Seek the Lord, with all my heart. Succeed in the home first and foremost. Be a person of integrity. Hear both sides. Pursue wise counsel. Be courageous and try new things. Develop a new skill each year. Creatively plan ahead. Keep my attitude positive and uplifting. Have a good sense of humor. Be organized at home and at work. Listen twice as much as I speak. Help others succeed.

My mission is to make a difference in other people's lives while living a life of integrity. *To fulfill my mission:*
I possess love: I freely give out love to those around me.
I inspire: I teach others that we are all deeply loved children of God. The 'Goliaths' in our lives *can be* vanquished!
I impact others: My thoughts, words and actions truly make a difference in people's lives.
I'm dedicated: I commit my time, talent and treasure to the accomplishment of my mission.
These are the roles I will fulfill in achieving my mission:
Child of God — God can count on me to keep following him and honor the promises I have made.
Husband — My wife is the M.I.P. (Most Important Person) in my life. We are a team together with God. "A cord of three strands is not quickly broken."
Father — I am 'there' for my children and enjoy teaching them about life and how to get the most out of each situation.
Family Member — I support and help my extended family.
Neighbor — The love of God is evident through my caring actions toward others.

My mission is to give, for giving is what I do best. I will seek to learn, for learning fosters growth and growing is the key to success. I will seek first to understand and find value in others. Value is the basis for respect, decisions and action. This will be the first step I take with my spouse, my family and my business. I want to influence the future development of individuals and organizations. I want to teach my children and others to love, laugh, learn and grow, beyond their current levels.

Action Plan

My Goal:
Lose twenty pounds in time for my class reunion.

What will I miss out on if I don't reach this goal?
The opportunity to look my best. I won't enjoy the "You look great!" comments

from my classmates.

What great things will happen as a result of reaching this goal?
I'll feel better about myself.

I'll develop the good habits of healthy eating and regularly exercising.

Obstacle	Solutions
Not enough time.	Get rid of low value time wasters.
	Re-prioritize activities.

Obstacle	Solutions
Not disciplined enough with	Make the choice to be consistent.
eating or exercising	Be accountable to my family.

Obstacle	Solutions
Easy to eat wrong foods due to	Prepare for my snacks and meals ahead
their accessibility.	of time. Always have good foods handy
	to snack on.

Worksheet

Today's Date: _____ *January 1*

Target Completion: _____ *June 7*

My Goal Faith Reminder:

Actual Completion: _____ *June 6*

I feel absolutely tremendous weighing in at 165 pounds! My new clothes fit

perfectly and I look great!

My Solution Faith Reminders:

I enjoy spending my time on high-value items.

It feels great being consistent with my eating and exercising.

I am disciplined with my eating and exercising.

I love being accountable to my family, and I keep my commitments.

It feels terrific being prepared with tasty, nutritious snacks to eat whenever I'm hungry.

Action Item	Eval. Date/Transfer Date			
Cut out one T.V. program each day.	Jan. 7	✓	Jan. 1	✓
Read the newspaper later, after exercise.	Jan. 7	✓	Jan. 1	✓

Action Item	Eval. Date/Transfer Date			
Schedule the exercise as a priority on my	Jan. 7	✓	Jan. 1	✓
calendar. Tell my spouse and kids of my	Jan. 7	✓	Jan. 1	✓
commitment. Have them ask me how I'm				
doing each day with my goal.				

Action Item	Eval. Date/Transfer Date			
Plan each week's menu on Sunday.	Jan. 7	✓	Jan. 1	✓
Prepare healthy snacks each day.	Jan. 3	✓	Jan. 1	✓
e.g. carrot sticks, celery sticks & fruit.				

Change Process Worksheet

1. List the attitude and/or habit you really want to change.
   I want to stop being so impatient.

2. What is the positive opposite of this attitude and/or habit?
   (e.g. impatient – patient, disorganized – organized).
   Impatient — Patient.

3. How did you develop this attitude in the first place? What events happened in your life? What things were said to you?
   As I grew up, the people around me were all very impatient. The more impatient they were with me, the less patience I had for anyone else.

4. Knowing that an attitude is a habit pattern of thinking; what thoughts do you want to change that are linked to the negative attitude you want to replace?
   When something doesn't go my way, I can relax, take a deep breath and stay calm. I will think peaceful thoughts and remember that "all things work for good."

5. Get leverage on yourself:
   a. What will happen if you don't change this attitude and the resulting behavior? What pain will you experience:

      This year: *My children will model my wrong behavior.*

      In five years: *My friends might choose to stay away.*

      In ten years: *My grandchildren will be negatively affected.*

   b. What great things will happen as a result of making the change? What joy and pleasure will it bring into your life:

      This year: *My children will learn how to be patient.*

      In five years: *My friends will enjoy being around me and feel at ease.*

      In ten years: *My grandchildren will love being with me and enjoy the freedom to make mistakes.*

6. Write out a 'faith reminder' with you already having accomplished the change and lock on to it.
   I am a patient, peaceful and relaxed person. People love being around me!

About the Author

Kevin Baerg founded Inspiration Press in 1994 to be a source of inspiration and hope for all of God's people. His first book, "Created for Excellence" has sold over 25,000 copies. He has presented the 'Keys to True Success' before thousands of people around the United States and Canada.

His 'training' started with seven years of service in Youth With A Mission (YWAM), teaching and working with people in Europe, Mexico, Canada and the United States.

He followed that with six years in the business community, including four years with one of America's leading human development training firms, Edge Learning Institute.

In 1993, Kevin stepped back into ministry with an eighteen month interim position as an Associate Pastor of one of the fastest growing churches in the Northwest United States.

He has also recently served as the Executive Director of Marriage Plus and is the host and a guest teacher on Ray Mossholder's "Singles Plus" television series.

Kevin teaches seminars around North America, challenging people to fulfill their potential in every area of life.

You'll enjoy his special blend of enthusiasm, humor and sincerity as he partners with God to impact people with powerful, life-changing principles as an author and a presenter.

Kevin and his wife Patty, along with their teenage children, Sarah and Tim, reside in beautiful Washington State.